# QUALITATIVE RESEARCH
# AND COMPLEX TEAMS

**SERIES IN UNDERSTANDING STATISTICS**
S. NATASHA BERETVAS    Series Editor

**SERIES IN UNDERSTANDING MEASUREMENT**
S. NATASHA BERETVAS    Series Editor

**SERIES IN UNDERSTANDING QUALITATIVE RESEARCH**
PATRICIA LEAVY    Series Editor

**Understanding Statistics**
*Exploratory Factor Analysis*
Leandre R. Fabrigar and
Duane T. Wegener

*Validity and Validation*
Catherine S. Taylor

**Understanding Measurement**
*Item Response Theory*
Christine DeMars

*Reliability*
Patrick Meyer

**Understanding Qualitative Research**
*Autoethnography*
Tony E. Adams, Stacy Holman Jones,
and Carolyn Ellis

*Qualitative Interviewing*
Svend Brinkmann

*Evaluating Qualitative
Research: Concepts, Practices, and
Ongoing Debates*
Jeasik Cho

*Qualitative Research and
Complex Teams*
Judith Davidson

*Video as Method*
Anne M. Harris

*Ethnography*
Anthony Kwame Harrison

*Focus Group Discussions*
Monique M. Hennink

*The Internet*
Christine Hine

*Oral History*
Patricia Leavy

*Using Think-Aloud Interviews and
Cognitive Labs in Educational Research*
Jacqueline P. Leighton

*Qualitative Disaster Research*
Brenda D. Phillips

*Fundamentals of Qualitative Research*
Johnny Saldaña

*Duoethnography*
Richard D. Sawyer and Joe Norris

*Analysis of the Cognitive Interview in
Questionnaire Design*
Gordon B. Willis

JUDITH DAVIDSON

# QUALITATIVE RESEARCH AND COMPLEX TEAMS

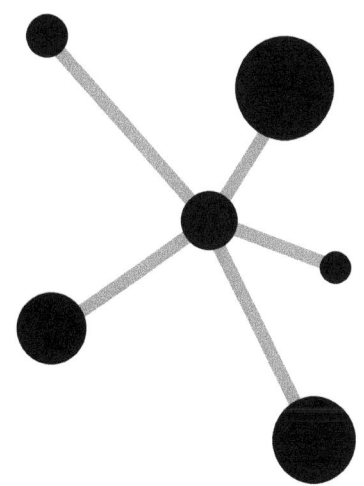

Oxford University Press is a department of the University of Oxford. It furthers
the University's objective of excellence in research, scholarship, and education
by publishing worldwide. Oxford is a registered trade mark of Oxford University
Press in the UK and certain other countries.

Published in the United States of America by Oxford University Press
198 Madison Avenue, New York, NY 10016, United States of America.

© Oxford University Press 2019

All rights reserved. No part of this publication may be reproduced, stored in
a retrieval system, or transmitted, in any form or by any means, without the
prior permission in writing of Oxford University Press, or as expressly permitted
by law, by license, or under terms agreed with the appropriate reproduction
rights organization. Inquiries concerning reproduction outside the scope of the
above should be sent to the Rights Department, Oxford University Press, at the
address above.

You must not circulate this work in any other form
and you must impose this same condition on any acquirer.

Library of Congress Cataloging-in-Publication Data
Names: Davidson, Judith, author.
Title: Qualitative research and complex teams / Judith Davidson.
Description: New York : Oxford University Press, [2019] |
Includes bibliographical references and index.
Identifiers: LCCN 2018012942 | ISBN 9780190648138 (pbk)
Subjects: LCSH: Qualitative research. | Qualitative research—Methodology. |
Research teams.
Classification: LCC H62 .D25425 2018 | DDC 001.4/2—dc23
LC record available at https://lccn.loc.gov/2018012942

# CONTENTS

Acknowledgments . . . . . . . . . . . . . . vii

INTRODUCTION  Why This Book Is Needed Now . . . . . . . . . . . . . . . . . . . . . 1

CHAPTER 1  Complex Research Teams on the Rise . . . . . . . . . . . . . 13

CHAPTER 2  Research Design in Team-Based Qualitative Research . . . . . . . . 39

CHAPTER 3  Writing Up Methods in Team-Based Qualitative Research . . . . . . . 71

CHAPTER 4  Substantive Writing in Team-Based Qualitative Research . . . . . . . 93

CHAPTER 5  Trends, Issues, and Considerations . . . . . . . . . . . . . . 119

Appendices . . . . . . . . . . . . . . . . 135
A  Example of Methodological Writing: Focus Group—How to Conduct . . . . . . . . . 135
B  Focus Group: Ground Rules . . . . . . . . 139
C  Example of a Methodological Log . . . . . . 141
D  Example of an Event Log . . . . . . . . . 143
E  Example of Methodological Coding . . . . . 145
F  Example of E-Project from the Top Down: Overview of Coding Section of a Project . . . . 147

G  Example of a Qualitative Research Syllabus: Team-Based Perspective . . . . . . . . . . . 149
H  Example of a Qualitative Research Course Schedule: Team-Based Perspective . . . . . . 163

Index . . . . . . . . . . . . . . . . 177

# ACKNOWLEDGMENTS

There is a certain irony in producing a single-author book on the topic of collaborative processes. However, as these acknowledgments illustrate, my work was actually supported by a large cast of necessary individuals and groups to whom I owe deep thanks. These include:

Liora Bresler, with whom I began the conversation about the Interpretive Zone when I was in my doctoral program at the University of Illinois.

Patricia Leavy, editor of this series, and supporter of qualitative researchers par excellence—thank you.

The wonderful group at the Oxford University Press must be thanked.

Collaborators from many team projects over the years— Chip Bruce, Elizabeth McNamara, Andy Harris, and Shanna Thompson—and many, many others.

My University of Massachusetts-Lowell colleagues located in many campus corners, from the faculty and staff of the College of Education to the Center for Program Evaluation, the Center for Women and Work, and the Qualitative Research Network.

The entire library staff at UMass Lowell deserve a special call-out for their willingness to support my many requests for materials.

The "Through Their Eyes" Project and the two qualitative research classes who participated in that team experiment deserve special recognition, as well as Ann Dean, director of the First Year Writing Program; Jeffrey VanderVeen, writing instructor; and Stephanie Lane, Jill Ramey, and Christy Whittlesey—doctoral students who took special roles in the work. Last but not least, thanks to Patrice Olivar, my undergraduate emerging scholar (2015–2016).

Some of the ideas raised here were presented in some form or another at the International Congress on Qualitative Inquiry (ICQI). Thank you, Trena Paulus and Kristi Jackson, friends and founders of the ICQI Digital Tools Special Interest group, for the resources and good thinking you have shared over the years.

Silvana di Gregorio, co-author on many pieces related to qualitative research and digital tools, continues to be an important part of my thinking about the issues discussed in this text.

Special thanks also to Sarah Kuhn, colleague and friend, who provided great time-outs when my brain was too cluttered.

Bob, my faithful friend and husband: You are an inspiration! Thank you for your good humor and kindness.

# QUALITATIVE RESEARCH
AND COMPLEX TEAMS

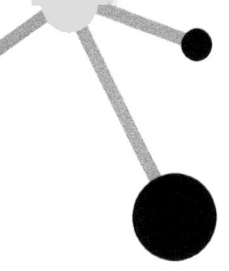

# INTRODUCTION

## *Why This Book Is Needed Now*

### Higher Education

Qualitative research methods were at the heart of the Documenting Effective Educational Practices (DEEP) project, "[A] two year study of 20 colleges and universities conducted over an 18-month period by a 24-member research team," designed to identify effective practices that would insure success for students in higher education (Kinzie et al., 2007, p. 971).

### K-12 Education and Community Youth Services

How do teenagers, teen caregivers, and others who work with teens perceive the reasons teens "sext" (send sexually explicit text messages)? This was the question driving a three-state, three-university, multidisciplinary qualitative research study using focus group and survey data from 123 teens, 92 parents, and 117 others in teen lives (Harris et al., 2013; Davidson, 2014).

### Health Services

A health project formed from two teams—a United States hospital team composed of nurses and researchers in midwifery, and a Dominican Republican hospital team composed of nurses from maternity work and doctors—joined forces with lay community workers doing outreach in four neighborhoods in the urban area near a Dominican hospital to better understand how to improve the chances of pregnant women with potentially dangerous obstetrical issues. Using qualitative research techniques, the two teams have worked together since 2004 to address this issue (Foster et al., 2012).

## Trends, Challenges, and Project Carcasses

There are three common elements to each of these project examples:

- They employ qualitative research,
- They are composed of multiple members, and,
- They display complex disciplinary, institutional, geographical, and other variables.

Taken as a whole, what you have here is complex qualitative team research. The examples cited here illustrate the growing trend that is seen across all forms of research, including qualitative research, toward increasingly complex research designs and more complex research teams.

The trend toward complexity in research has significant implications for all stages of research work—from research design through the final product. Looking specifically at qualitative research, the challenges raised come at a time when our understanding about the writing-up of research is also coming under strong scrutiny by those within the field (Clerke & Hopwood, 2014).

As we move into this new era, we lack much of the basic methodological information we need to understand how to operate in these new circumstances. Qualitative researchers, and those who work with them, have not had clear instructions on, or adequate experience in, integrating giving attention to the theory and practice of qualitative research with new considerations of writing in a team-based setting. This means that in many project settings, leaders and members are flying blind or with only a limited view of what is ahead. This is dangerous and could negatively affect every stage of a project, from research design and team formation, to data collection and analysis.

Even researchers with extensive qualitative research background and knowledge of the latest developments in writing in this field may not fully understand how to work with complex, interdisciplinary teams at the level that is needed to successfully complete such a project. This deficit is in part related to the longstanding tradition of teaching qualitative research as if most studies were conducted by single researchers working alone in the field. For many people, qualitative research is still represented by the image of one lone anthropologist working in a distant village or on an island. These are not the circumstances under which we work today, and yet, for the most part, our teaching materials and instructional lessons still present qualitative research as a solitary endeavor.

These problematic strands all come together when you look at the range of products any given research team is able to produce. Time and again, as a researcher, teacher, and consultant, I find that lack of understanding about qualitative research, writing, or team collaboration leads to "dead projects." Dead projects are those that were conceived and conducted (meaning data were collected and a report was written), but after that, there is no more use made of the project materials and findings, which are filed and left to rot like a dead carcass. These "project carcasses" can be found in computers, file cabinets, closets, and thumb drives—anywhere out of the way where you probably won't step on them, and you won't have to smell them.

When researchers admit to these dead projects in their pasts, they are usually embarrassed, unhappy with themselves, and wondering why they didn't know how to do a better job with the materials. They are apologetic about the data they collected, feeling they didn't meet the expectations of the study participants, research collaborators, and their own professional standards. They know the potential of their work did not come to fruition. To be a good researcher is to make good use of the opportunity of doing research and the materials that are collected by developing the richest possible set of interpretations and sharing them appropriately with other audiences. When this doesn't happen, you have failed research—and project carcasses.

The purpose of this book is to help researchers move through and beyond this challenge, making sure each team-based qualitative research project is able to be all it can be, producing good products representing a full and deep understanding of the issue(s) under study. In other words, my mission is to stop the proliferation of project carcasses!

## How and Why I Came to This Issue

My interest in the issue of complex teams in qualitative research was piqued when I realized how many team projects I had participated in as a qualitative researcher, but how little methodological literature I had encountered on this topic. In my graduate school at the University of Illinois in Urbana–Champaign, Illinois, this included: (a) Liora Bresler's team of doctoral students studying arts in elementary schools (Wasser & Bresler, 1996); (b) Daniel Walsh's team of doctoral students studying a unique preschool setting; (c) a team project sponsored by the university's Center for the Study of Reading, examining adolescent readers with special needs; and (d) Bruce's study of an inquiry-based science and math methods course for teacher education candidates (Bruce & Davidson, 1996). In fact, like most graduate students, I can attest that the only major research project I worked on primarily by myself was my dissertation (Davidson, 2000).

Post-graduation, my experience followed a similar path. I was part of a number of research collaborations, from the Hanau Model School Partnership at TERC in Cambridge, Massachusetts (Davidson, 2003; Davidson & Olson, 2003); to the project examining views about teen sexting mentioned at the beginning of this chapter, which I will refer to from here on out as "The Sexting Project" (Harris et al., 2013). These experiences led me to deeper understanding of research design for teams, the role of the qualitative researcher on a complex team, and the issues related to writing up research in which multiple researchers have been involved.

Ironically, even though I had written about issues related to the conduct of team research (Wasser & Bresler, 1996, Wasser, McGillivray, & McNamara, 1998), as a teacher of qualitative research methods, I, like others, taught my students to undertake research as individuals, not as collaborative group members. I did it this way because this is how I was taught and how most textbooks approached the subject.

Not too many years ago, my dissatisfaction with the lack of attention to teams among qualitative researchers and within qualitative research instruction reached a critical mass. I noticed that on my campus and beyond, the landscape was changing. Increasingly, requests for proposals from government, private agencies, and within the university emphasized the need for interdisciplinary collaborations. As my department embarked on development of a new doctorate in the area of Research Methods and Program Evaluation in Education, we took this opportunity to shift many of our student research experiences toward collaborative teamwork to ensure that our graduates would have the skills they needed after graduation to be successful on interdisciplinary teams.

At the same time, the field of qualitative research had for some time been challenging traditional ways of writing in research, and these changes in perspectives on writing had important implications for the conduct of team research. As a former literacy specialist with experience in teaching writing to children and adults, I couldn't help but be intrigued by the conversations about writing arising in the world of qualitative research (Davidson, 2000). Standardized forms of social science representation, highly influenced by scientific models, were being enlarged and expanded upon by a growing number of non-standardized forms (Denzin & Lincoln, 2011; Pelias, 2011). This movement of change in the arena of writing up qualitative research was accelerated by the explosion of the Internet and new forms and formats of digital communication, from blogs and wikis to video streaming and YouTube (Davidson & di Gregorio, 2011). The idea for this book emerged as these streams of change converged, and I found myself being carried along by the current.

## The Heart and Focus of This Book

The overall goal of this book is to offer readers guidelines for working in this new research arena and with the new challenges it brings. From the perspective of qualitative researchers, this new space is imbued from start to finish with the power and importance of writing to the qualitative research endeavor. The aim of this book is to improve the likelihood that you, and your team, will be successful in conducting *and* writing up your research project.

This book is informed by my own hands-on experiences in this field and the increasingly rich sources of research information in regard to qualitative research, complex team functioning, and writing up qualitative research. Although the overall focus is on the needs of qualitative research teams, I would like to think there is much good information here that will also be of use to the researcher planning to conduct a research project on her or his own.

This book will provide you with answers to these questions and more:

- How can qualitative researchers position themselves to do their best on a complex qualitative team research project?
- What is the unique role writing plays in qualitative research, and how is the role of writing in qualitative research reshaped by the structure and demands of a complex research team?
- What is "methodological writing"? Why is it important to all parts of the project? How do you set yourself up to get the most from your methodological writing?
- What is "substantive writing"? How does writing help you to capture and explore your substantive findings? What are the ways to enrich its possibilities?
- What does the future hold for those who are working at the intersection between qualitative research and complex team projects?

## Definitions Used in This Volume

### Qualitative Research

When I use the term "qualitative research," I mean research on the human condition that is conducted through the study of "texts" (in the broadest meaning of that term), from an interpretive perspective, with the aim of getting at the inner life, consciousness, or meaning humans attribute to the situation.

### Complex Research Team

When I use the term "complex research team," I mean groups of four or more individuals working together on a research endeavor that may be in a specific geographic location, in virtual space, or in hybrid circumstances.

## Complex Qualitative Research Team

When I use the term "complex qualitative research team," I mean a complex research team conducting qualitative research on a defined topic or issue for a specific period of time. The team may employ qualitative research techniques solely, or use a mixture of quantitative and qualitative methods. Their collaboration aims toward project products in which writing or some other form of formal text creation is a dominant form for expressing the results of their learning.

## Project

When I use the term "project," I mean a

> temporary endeavor undertaken to create a unique product, service or result. A project is temporary in that it has a defined beginning and end in time, and therefore defined scope and resources. And a project is unique in that it is not a routine operation, but a specific set of operations designed to accomplish a singular goal. So a project team often includes people who don't usually work together—sometimes from different organizations and across multiple geographies. (From http://www.pmi.org/en/About-Us/About-Us-What-is-Project-Management.aspx)

In other words, a "project" is the work research teams do. Qualitative research is a methodological approach research teams might use. Writing is at the heart of what qualitative researchers do. When you combine these elements, you have complex qualitative research teams going about their inquiries and writing up their research.

## Who Will Gain from Reading This Book?

This book is an attempt to provide some guidelines and resources for researchers who are caught at the intersection between these two rivers of activity—the growth of complex qualitative team research and the changing understanding of writing in the social sciences.

This is a book that will answer the questions of a variety of audiences:

- Graduate and undergraduate students seeking to learn new research skills and how to be successful on a research project;
- Instructors in any academic area in which research team organization must be considered;
- Research leaders establishing a new project;
- Individuals working in nonprofit or for-profit organizations where one needs to know how to conduct qualitative research in team-based circumstances;
- Anyone engaged with qualitative research.

I do not assume my reader is an expert in qualitative research methodology. In my experience, most complex qualitative research teams are composed of a mix of individuals—from those with deep experience in the methodology to those with virtually none. My goal is for this text to be useful to both. For that reason, the chapter following this one provides the reader who is a beginner to qualitative research with a general background to the basics of qualitative research. Throughout the text, references and resources are meant to be useful both to beginners and to those who are more adept and knowledgeable about the methodology.

## Organization of This Book

This is one of a series of volumes addressing the issues of writing up qualitative research. Each volume in the series takes up another aspect of this complex task. This volume follows a similar structure to its siblings' in the series.

The introduction provides an overview of the issue the book will address—writing up research on qualitative research in complex teams—as well as important definitions that undergird discussions in the following chapters, an overview of what the book will contain, and consideration of how it might serve different readers' needs.

The first chapter provides a theoretical discussion of the issues that appear to be spurring an increase in the use of interdisciplinary teams around the world. This chapter also provides background on three important areas that will be useful to those who are novices to qualitative research: (1) overview of the small but growing literature about complex teams in qualitative research; (2) consideration of the changing understanding of writing in qualitative research; and (3) a basic primer on the principles of qualitative research and an introduction to forms of qualitative research.

The second chapter describes research design issues in complex teams, with special attention to the formation of such teams, ethical considerations teams must address ("internalized and externalized caring," as I refer to it), structuring of the qualitative research database the team will be using, and the role writing will play in the design and conduct of team-based research.

As an aside, it is not a coincidence that throughout the book, there is a strong emphasis on the writing process. My training and experience have led me to believe that the quality and success of the project will be determined by the quality and content of the writing process. For that reason, I provide detailed discussion of the intermediate processes that take place, whatever the final outcome achieved.

Chapter 3 focuses on writing and qualitative research methodology. I describe three areas of methodological writing that I feel team-based researchers should attend to: (1) *in process*, (2) *ideal*, and (3) *methodological literature*. The first term, *in process*, refers to the notion that qualitative research methodology is composed through writing, and writing about methodology in the process of doing research is therefore a requirement. The second term, *ideal*, is a reference to the emergent or standardized methodological description the team is always in the process of constructing to describe the way they conducted the inquiry up to that point. The third term, *methodological literature*, refers to the contribution each project can make to moving qualitative research methodology forward through thoughtful reflection and reporting on methodology.

Writing up research findings or reporting on the substantive knowledge of an inquiry is the focus of Chapter 4. It explores four distinct areas necessary to composing substantive texts, and the implications of each for team-based research. These are: doing and documenting interpretive work, testing for trustworthiness, determining the forms of reporting and kinds of writing, and ensuring the project's success.

The rise of complex research teams presents many new challenges for all researchers, and those challenges contain unique twists for qualitative researchers. In Chapter 5, I discuss a range of these challenges or trends and consider the implications they raise for qualitative researchers.

Several appendices follow the main text, with examples of many of the issues discussed in the book.

## Conclusion

Writing in its broadest sense—that is, the creation of texts documenting thoughts, ideas, impressions, and observations of human social life—is the heart and soul of qualitative research. Moreover, writing (again in the broadest sense we can construe) is central to the interpretive possibilities of any given inquiry. We forge our methodology through writing, and we share our ultimate understanding of an issue, situation, or case through multiple literacies.

If writing is meant as the creation of permanent and/or evanescent symbolic notations describing, reflecting upon, and coming to some sort of conclusion about a social problem of interest, then as humans, we "write" in many forms; with pen on paper; with computers; with our bodies arched in space; with paint on walls; and in plays, speaking words we have composed.

In this volume, I turn my sights to issues of writing that have concerned me as a qualitative researcher standing on the edge of a new, globalized, interdisciplinary, and digitalized world of inquiry. In this new world of inquiry, complex teams are on the rise, appearing in more and more contexts and disciplinary areas. I am excited by the new possibilities for collaboration, thinking, and sharing that this world brings. Writing that is sharing of what has been learned is a necessary part of collaborative inquiry. While it brings joy, excitement, and new insights, it is also a difficult path, fraught with potential tensions, and, as mentioned earlier—the unfortunate occasional project carcass. It is my hope that this volume will provide useful advice and comforting support for making one's way through these thickets.

### References

Bruce, Bertram C., and Judith Davidson. 1996. "An Inquiry Model for Literacy Across the Curriculum." *Journal of Curriculum Studies* 28 (3): 281–300.

Clerke, Teena, and Nick Hopwood. 2014. *Doing Ethnography in Teams: A Case Study of Asymmetries in Collaborative Research*. Springer Briefs in Education. Cham, the Netherlands: Springer.

Davidson, Judith. 2000. *Living Reading: Exploring the Lives of Reading Teachers*. Edited by Joe L. Kincheloe and Shirley R. Steinberg. Vol. 124, *Counterpoints: Studies in the Postmodern Theory of Education*. New York: Peter Lang.

Davidson, Judith. 2003. "A New Role in Facilitating School Reform: The Case of the Educational Technologist." *Teachers College Record* 105 (5): 729–752.

Davidson, Judith. 2014. *Sexting: Gender and Teens*. Edited by Patricia Leavy. Vol. 3, *Teaching Gender*. Rotterdam, Netherlands: Sense Publications.

Davidson, Judith, and Silvana di Gregorio. 2011. "Qualitative Research and Technology: In the Midst of a Revolution." In *The Sage Handbook of Qualitative Research*, edited by Norman K. Denzin and Yvonna S. Lincoln, 627–643. Los Angeles, CA: Sage Publications.

Davidson, Judith, and Matthew Olson. 2003. "School Leadership in Networked Schools: Deciphering the Impact of Large Technical Systems on Education." *International Journal of Leadership in Education* 6 (3): 261–281.

Denzin, Norman K., and Yvonna S. Lincoln, eds. 2011. *The Sage Handbook of Qualitative Research*. 4th ed. Los Angeles, CA: Sage Publications.

Foster, J. W., F. Chiang, R. I. Burgos, R. E. Cáceres, C. M. Tejada, A. T. Almonte, F. R. Noboa, L. J. Perez, M. F. Urbaez, and A. Heath. 2012. "Community-based Participatory Research and the Challenges of Qualitative Analysis Enacted by Lay, Nurse, and Academic Researchers." *Research in Nursing & Health* 35 (5): 550–559. 10p. doi:10.1002/nur.21494

Harris, Andrew J., Judith Davidson, Elizabeth Letourneau, Carl Paternite, and Karin Tusinski Miofsky. 2013. Building a Prevention Framework to Address Teen "Sexting" Behaviors. U.S. Department of Justice, Washington, DC.

Kinzie, Jillian, Peter Magolda, Adrianna Kezar, George Kuh, Sara Hinkle, and Elizabeth Whitt. 2007. "Methodological Challenges in Multi-Investigator Multi-Institutional Research in Higher Education." *Higher Education* 54 (3): 469–482. doi:10.1007/s10734-006-9007-7

Pelias, Ronald J. 2011. "Writing into Position: Strategies for Composition and Evaluation." In *The Sage Handbook of Qualitative Research*, edited by Norman K. Denzin and Yvonna S. Lincoln, 659–668. Thousand Oaks, CA: Sage Publications.

Wasser, Judith Davidson, and Liora Bresler. 1996. "Working in the Interpretive Zone: Conceptualizing Collaboration in Qualitative Research Teams." *Educational Researcher* 25 (5): 5–15.

Wasser, Judith Davidson, Kevin McGillivray, and Elizabeth McNamara. 1998. "Diaries of an Educational Technologist: A New Role for Technology Integration Support." *Hands-On* 21 (2).

# COMPLEX RESEARCH TEAMS ON THE RISE

THE IMAGE of the lonely researcher—projects conducted by a singleton researcher, or team research that is represented as an individual of sorts—is a longstanding tradition within qualitative research (Mauthner & Doucet, 2008; Rogers-Dillon, 2005; Siemens, Yin, & Smith, 2014; Wasser & Bresler, 1996). Despite this image, an increasing amount of qualitative research is conducted by teams.

There are many reasons why complex qualitative team research has come to the fore at this particular moment, but for the purposes of this narrative, I am going to focus here on the following set of concerns:

- Increased recognition of qualitative research;
- Globalization plus increased complexity of research problems;
- Interdisciplinarity and transdisciplinarity;
- Digitalization; and,
- Considerations of social justice: intersectionality and post-colonialism.

## Increased Recognition of Qualitative Research

The rise in large and complex research teams comes at a time when qualitative research methods are being accepted as legitimate modes for inquiry among serious social scientists (Hesse-Biber, Rodriguez, & Frost, 2015). This acceptance follows a long period during the 20th century, often called the "paradigm wars," in which quantitative and qualitative research were depicted as being at odds with each other (Hesse-Biber, 2015). On today's large, complex teams, qualitative research plays one of two roles: (1) it is the sole method employed, or (2) it is integrated with other modes of inquiry, as in mixed methods studies.

## Globalization Plus Complexity of Problems

"Globalization," referring to the rapid integration of economic, political, and cultural spaces, has led to increased collaboration within and across institutional boundaries ("Globalization," 2016). On one hand, global research has led to the development of multi-sited ethnographic work that takes as its focus the understanding of ideas, practices, roles, or other phenomena. On the other hand, team ethnography owes much to "changes in the academic mode of production" that favor large-scale and interdisciplinary work (Jarzabkowski, Bednarek, & Cabantous, 2015, p. 7).

Partnerships arising from globalization are diverse in nature, pairing the academy and industry, for-profit and non-profit organizations (Brocke & Lippe, 2015). Collaborative research projects formed by consortia of institutional partners "play a growing role in the portfolio of public and private organizations" (Brocke & Lippe, 2015, p. 1022). The number of participants, size of the budget, scale of activities, and outcome expectations surpass anything in which most qualitative researchers have previously participated.

Business researchers have found that widely distributed teams may need to adopt different practices than those found in smaller, more localized project work, paying particular attention to the ways members are acknowledged for their participation (Drouin & Bourgault, 2013).

## Interdisciplinarity and Transdisciplinarity

"Interdisciplinarity" and "transdisciplinarity" are two related terms representing different points on the same continuum.

Interdisciplinarity (working at the intersection among disciplines) refers to multiple disciplinary partners interacting with each other, and, in the process, creating new forms of knowledge about the topic and practice of inquiry (Haythornthwaite, 2006; Repko & Szostak, 2017). Leavy states that "interdisciplinarity turns into transdisciplinarity in a given project via transcendence and deep levels of collaboration" (Leavy, 2011, p. 24). Despite the shift towards merging or working across boundaries in academic spaces, disciplines possess vastly different understandings about collaboration that are rooted in institutional history and can be described as the differences between "equity of academic control" and "degree of disciplinary difference" (Siemens, Yin, & Smith, 2014, p. 53). These issues—the merging of diverse individuals and ideas—are at the heart of the work undertaken by large, complex research teams. They are considerations across the timeline of the project, with significant implications for the results of the writing up and reporting of the work.

## Digitalization

The rise of the internet has provided researchers with both new tools *and* new content and topics for inquiry. As electrical impulses whiz around the world, digital technologies have changed the scope of many inquiries from local to global. Methodological texts are beginning to absorb these changes and respond with descriptions of new techniques grounded in Internet use (Salmons, 2016; Paulus, Lester, & Dempster, 2014).

Thanks to these technological changes, it is now possible to conduct much inquiry from one's local position, without travelling the world. There is also growing recognition that internet practices are objects of inquiry, and, moreover that internet practices are intricately connected to daily face-to-face contexts ("Why We Post," 2016).

Qualitative researchers have been in the thick of these and related technical developments as they search for methods to improve the quality of their inquiries—from the adoption of tape recorders and cameras, to the implementation of Qualitative Data Analysis Software (QDAS) and the introduction of digital ethnography (Davidson & di Gregorio, 2011; di Gregorio & Davidson, 2008; Davidson, Paulus, & Jackson, 2016).

## Considerations of Social Justice: Intersectionality and Post-Colonialism

A final consideration that is closely related to each of the previous considerations is the changing understanding of the relationship of researcher to "researchee" (subject), which is related to our deepening knowledge of the effects of multiple forms of oppression, including race, class, gender, language, and ethnicity (Dutta, 2014, 2016; Sanford & Angel-Ajani, 2006). These forms of oppression are related to the imposition of colonialism, particularly in its most recent form as the dominance of the Northern hemisphere over the Southern hemisphere of the globe. For qualitative researchers, this has meant that the United States and Europe had temporary dominance over the field, but this circumstance is changing (Mohanty, 2003).

Taken together, these five impulses form the background to the rise in complex qualitative research teams. No one thing alone can be called upon to account for this dramatic change in research style, but taken together, they have had a profound effect on turning the tide from individualistic to collective focused research in the social sciences in general, and in qualitative research in particular.

## Complex Qualitative Research Teams

In making the shift from the focus on individually conducted qualitative research, "the social science community has been mostly unreflexive and uncritical in its adoption of team-based research models and practices, and there appears to be an unspoken assumption that team research is 'better' than solo research" (Mauthner & Doucet, 2008, p. 972). As we move to a more reflexive stance, it is critical that we understand the foundation from which we are starting, which is the small but growing body of research on complex qualitative research teams and the larger, but often misunderstood, body of research on writing in qualitative research. The emerging literature on complex qualitative research teams can be divided into two interwoven arenas: (1) information on the structural issues that accompany the move into teamwork; and (2) discussion of the processual issues related to conduct of the project.

## Structural Issues in Complex Qualitative Research Teams

Literature about structural concerns in complex qualitative research teams has paid attention to the issues of membership, role, integration, and scaling up. In regard to membership, an important starting point is who composes the membership of the team—meaning who comes together, and why they choose to join the project. Another pertinent question for a large team is: "How is the whole structured in relationship to the parts, and, in particular, what role do qualitative researchers play on the team?" Reviewing the structural descriptions of complex qualitative research teamwork, I found myself in awe of the intricate team structures researchers reported in the literature. These same accounts provide important information about the challenges that occur with scaling up from individual projects to large-team work.

While the size of the teams employing qualitative researchers has increased, we have yet to fully understand "the dynamics of multi-investigator multi-institutional projects" (Kinzie et al. 2007, p. 369). This group of 24 higher-education researchers working across 20 higher-education institutions found that creating a cohesive team required significant work bridging members' philosophical differences, addressing issues related to data collection and analysis, as well as working efficiently and appropriately with diverse field sites. No less complicated was the task of writing up the team-based results for different audiences.

"Representational groups" is a term introduced by Curry et al. (2012) to describe the ways teams, through diverse membership, bring into juxtaposition different organizations, professional groups, methodological beliefs, and identity groups. They used intergroup relationship theory to explore the tensions team members face and to suggest solutions.

A number of researchers have pointed to the ways complex qualitative research teams divide roles within the team. Some teams follow the well-worn path of hierarchical team research: that is, where one lead researcher oversees a legion of research assistants, often graduate students; but others create more egalitarian structures (Rogers-Dillon, 2005). Liggett et al. (1994), in their work on a three-year multi-site policy study examining issues of mainstreaming and special education children, reported creating a lead team of four members that drew upon a secondary level of ad hoc team members ranging from qualitative researchers to special education advocates and legal experts. This allowed them to combine top-level theoretical opinions and ground-level practice in their work with 18 sites—6 states and 12 school districts. With access and advice provided by the secondary level team, the four lead team members conducted a total of 350 interviews, as well as combing through numerous documents.

Liggett et al. (1994) raised the issue of teams of insider/outsiders, which in their case took the form of a fairly formal model resembling a traditional advisory board. Increasing numbers of researchers, however, are working in much more radically participatory models that engage researchees as partners in the search for knowledge. Going under titles such as Community-Based Participatory Research (CBPR), they seek authentic engagement with "the other." This was the approach taken by Foster et al. (Foster et al. 2012) in the cross-cultural study mentioned in the opening of this chapter. In this study of pregnancy care in the Dominican Republic, U.S. and Dominican health professionals sought to work in an egalitarian manner that actively engaged community members in democratic discussion of issues related to why women in this area were not getting faster care for potentially complicated pregnancies. Their attention to equal participation in the study meant changes in all components of the research design, from data collection to analysis, and including the writing and presenting of study results.

The more traditional hierarchical model was also challenged by Mauthner and Doucet (2008), who turned to Bourdieu's theory of epistemic reflexivity as a tool for problematizing the issues facing academic teams. They argue that this is done "by critically examining collective and normative team-based research relationships and practices as ways of constructing knowledge" (Mauthner & Doucet, 2008, p. 973).

As this short review demonstrates, the options for organizing the work of complex teams are many, and each decision about structure will impact issues related to writing on every dimension.

## Processual Issues in Complex Qualitative Research Teams

The literature on processual issues in complex qualitative research teams provides information on how teams make meaning within those structures. Processual issues are particularly pronounced for team-based researchers, and qualitative researchers have spent significant time and paper examining the ways by which these issues affect interpretation, and, thus, writing.

My personal entry into these discussions began in a paper in which I described the concept of "the interpretive zone" (Wasser & Bresler, 1996). In this article, Liora Bresler and I reported on a multi-year qualitative research study of arts instruction in elementary schools (dance, music, and visual arts) conducted by a team composed of a faculty leader (Bresler) and four doctoral students (of which I—Wasser, now Davidson, was one). In this piece, we described how meaning making was located in team processes.

We defined the interpretive zone in these ways:

> The interpretive zone is the place where multiple viewpoints are held in dynamic tension as a group seeks to make sense of fieldwork issues and meanings. (Wasser & Bresler, 1996, p. 6)

> We use this term to indicate the mental location where interpretation takes place.... In the interpretive zone, researchers bring together their different kinds of knowledge, experience, and beliefs to forge new meanings through the process of the joint inquiry in which they are engaged. (Wasser & Bresler, 1996, p. 13)

In defining this term, we were emphatic that we meant it to refer to collective, not merely individualistic, processes of meaning-making, and we pointed to the importance of "developing meta awareness of group as interpretive tool" (Wasser & Bresler, 1996, p. 11).

It was also our belief that the term "interpretive zone" was equally weighted between the two words—*interpretive* and *zone*, although Bresler and I were intrigued by the many notions raised by the word *zone*, identifying examples of the idea of zone from psychology, linguistics, and military action. In the end, we chose to liken the interpretive zone to the tidal area along the shore of an ocean where waves move back and forth, covering and exposing the beach across the hours of the day and night. This stretch of sand or rock can be turbulent or calm, wet and flooded or parched and drying out. It takes special skills for an organism to do well in this environment, and those that have adapted are unique in their persistence and endurance. This was the image of *zone* we felt best described our understanding of the place where collaborative work occurs and meanings are made. (A note of self-disclosure: At the time I selected this term, I had also been recently reintroduced to the book *Between Pacific Tides* by John Steinbeck's marine biologist chum Edward Ricketts [Ricketts & Calvin, 1968], and the title and the ocean images did play a role in my choice of words!)

Reviewing this earlier article, I realize much of what I describe in this book in regard to formative writing for methodological or interpretive purposes grows from these initial discussions with Liora Bresler, mentor and friend. For instance, we described the importance of interpretive meetings and interpretive writing (referring to formative memos written early in the project chronology). We noted in our accounting of our own processes that preparation for interpretive meetings becomes increasingly time-consuming as the project continues and data and interpretations accumulate.

Our work was spurred by concern that there was a lack of thick description regarding collaborative interpretive processes, and as a result, these processes were not yet well understood. Our call was heeded, and between then and now, research in this area has increased.

Anders and Lester (2015) provide in-depth description of the complexities of analyzing and writing up research conducted across disciplinary boundaries. In a study of Burundian refugees in the United States conducted by a joint team of educational and health researchers, they found that disciplinary lenses led them to have different expectations of key concepts they had presumed to be shared, and these differences led in turn to differences about what was a finding (Anders & Lester, 2015). These researchers were surprised to find that what they had perceived to be neutral methodological or disciplinary concepts were often historically contextualized in a colonial past. "Others have highlighted how contemporary research methodologies, many of which are steeped in Western culture, have resulted in colonizing practices and (mis)understanding" (Anders & Lester, 2015, p. 747). Creating a shared understanding among researchers meant backtracking to antecedent concepts that could be identified as existing prior to the diverging paths of assumption taken by different disciplinary groups. Juxtaposing the U.S. and Burundian beliefs also helped to get beneath the obstacles presented by disciplinary differences.

The struggle to make sense of analysis in complex qualitative research teams is a theme echoed by many authors. Döös and Wilhelmson (2014) examine the elusive notion of intersubjectivity as a construct with which group analysis must struggle. Proximity was particularly important to supporting the development of intersubjectivity, and, thus, the team's ability to communicate as they conducted analytical activities. In their case, "proximity" referred to intense data collection coupled with ongoing discussion of the unfolding meaning in which development of metaphorical descriptions lead to theoretical insights. Doos and Wilhelmson refer to the more (a team of four) as opposed to the different (multiple researchers of different stripes), which may raise significant challenges to their discussion of intersubjectivity.

Intersubjectivity, as a means of understanding human interactions within the interpretive zone, is also a significant consideration in the work of Gerstl-Pepin and Gunzenhauser (2002), as they raise issues related to theoretical notions of feminist postmodernism, dialogue, and performance as factors in team-based functioning. Paulus, Woodside, and Ziegler (2008) coined the term "dialogic collaborative process" in discussing the analysis component of complex qualitative team research. Their work emphasizes the importance of examining the horizontal aspect of teamwork, as well as the vertical or hierarchical.

The notion of collaboration itself is taken up in Gershon's edited volume, in which he notes that while much qualitative research has been conducted by groups of researchers, it has been less common to describe "the ways in which co-authors worked together or . . . [t]he implicit and explicit collaborations between 'researcher' and 'researched'" (Gershon, 2009, xvii). He links the lack of attention to these two forms of collaboration among researchers and researchers and participants to both the inward turn in qualitative research (self-reflections) and attention to arts-based research approaches. Interestingly, these two movements are also contributing over time to a return to reflection on collaboration.

Core to the process of making meaning in qualitative research (for individuals or for teams) is the act of writing, the topic of the next section.

## Writing in Qualitative Research

Qualitative researchers truly write to think—it is our unique blessing and curse. Our interpretive approaches rely significantly on texts that others create for us, we create about others, and we create in reflection. We are engaged in language and writing throughout a project. Our acts of analysis require us to create language to describe language, images, and experiences.

Our experience writing, and our interest in thinking through writing make us excellent partners on a collaborative research project—whether it be completely qualitative or mixed methods. However, careful planning, knowledge, and strategy are needed to insure our writing skills are used to the greatest benefit and in the most effective manner.

The central role of writing in the conduct of qualitative research has made it a major discussion point in the arena of qualitative research. In the last few decades, qualitative researchers have given much thought and attention to writing—its forms and impact.

In the 1980s, social scientists became aware of themselves as producers of texts of different genres, and they thought hard about the implications of pouring ideas into these vessels (Geertz, 1973; Clifford & Marcus, 1986; Wolf, 1992; Richardson, 1994). Developments from these insights have led to significant experimentation in qualitative research writing, as a world opened up in which social scientists sought to understand how the meaning would change if the form changed (Richardson, 1994; Ellis, 2004).

Today, a new generation of qualitative researchers is building upon these critiques with views that challenge multiple facets related to the writing up of research (Lather, 2013; Lather & St. Pierre, 2013; Pierre, 2014; St. Pierre, 2012; Taylor & Ivinson, 2013). Describing themselves as "the post-posts," meaning those who come after post-structuralism and/or post-modernism, this new circle of qualitative researchers builds upon the insights of their foremothers (or -fathers) into the new possibilities for qualitative research writing, while at the same time challenging hidden assumptions the field continues to make in regard to content (what can we write about) and form (what will that writing look like). Integrated with this exploration has been interest in the role the arts could play in qualitative research. Many qualitative researchers began to experiment with forms identified as arts-based research (Bresler, 2004; Davidson, 2004; Barone & Eisner, 2012; Leavy, 2009; Knowles & Cole, 2008; Faulkner, 2009). These experiments provided new avenues for the representation of knowledge derived from qualitative research inquiries. In addition to the experiments that opened new ground for exploration, there were also scholars who undertook the important work of integration of these approaches into the bones of qualitative research—design and representation (Ely et al., 1997).

Qualitative researchers became aware of the need and possibility to communicate with different audiences, particularly those outside of academia who would not be interested in reading works written in scholarly genre. Thus were developed such forms as social fictions ("Social Fictions Series," 2017) as well as ethnopoetics, performance ethnography, and other forms of arts-based research (Knowles & Cole, 2008; Denzin, 2003).

The growth in interest in fictional and creative nonfiction as tools for qualitative research writing occurred at the same time the English community was developing a parallel interest in understanding the structure and processes of collaborative writing. Discussions regarding the nature of collaborative writing had been percolating for some time before they emerged as a full-blown conversation in the late 1980s and early 1990s, encompassing English and other fields. Argument about the role of social interaction in learning and practice, which can be tracked back to the pedagogical ideas of Dewey, Mead, and Piaget, were at the heart of these concerns (Ede & Lunsford, 1990; LeFevre, 1987).

Today, there is intense study of collaborative writing work as it is undertaken in many different kinds of workplaces, from business and medicine to government, policy, journalism, administration (Van Steendam, 2016; Colen & Petelin, 2004). This work makes manifest the diverse forms collaborative writing can take (Lowry, Curtis, & Lowry, 2004; Couture, 1989). A particular concern of scholars is the challenges interdisciplinarity raises for collaborative writing activities (Palmeri, 2004).

Another shift in qualitative research that has had an effect on the conduct and writing up of research is the change in relationship from subject to participant, to, in some cases, protagonist (Dutta, 2016; Sanford & Angel-Ajani, 2006). This shift has led to increased roles for the "research other" in all phases of the research.

Today, it would be fair to say that qualitative research writing falls into two camps that I will refer to by the terms *scientific style writing* and *creative social science writing*. (These two approaches are addressed in much greater depth in Chapter 4.)

## What Is Missing: What Is Needed

Returning to the guiding theme of this text—writing up qualitative research on complex teams—what has been missing from the methodological literature has been attention to the mechanics or details of large-scale work, including the leadership, organization, and technologies required to undertake such endeavors. Much of the literature is about the experiences of single researchers working alone. This was the assumed norm, and it was up to researchers working on teams to translate that work to their various situations.

In similar fashion, while the growing body of work on composition in qualitative research has done a good job of charting new creative territory, there is now a great need to translate the findings from this work into the nuts and bolts of large-scale teamwork, integrating thinking about teams with thinking about the challenges of writing collaboratively.

These considerations form the goal of this book—to provide frontline research leaders and workers, whether qualitatively or otherwise oriented—with detailed information on how complex research projects can be designed and conducted to make the best use of qualitative research perspectives and knowledge of writing practice for better ends—meaning richer, more thoughtful, trustworthy, and useful final products. In pursuit of this goal, the next section of this chapter provides basic information on qualitative research—definition, principles, and a framework for understanding the forms of qualitative research data. This is included for the reader who is not familiar with qualitative research, but it may also be useful for readers who want to locate the approach to qualitative research taken within this book.

## What Is Qualitative Research, and What Can It Contribute to Complex Research Projects?

### Defining Qualitative Research

From a strictly technical perspective, qualitative research is defined by its primary source of information, texts that have not been converted into restricted or purely numerical forms, and its approach to interpretation that, in parallel fashion, does not reduce the analysis of these materials to restricted or numerical forms (Punch & Oancea, 2014). By "texts" I mean not only written texts (such as published books and handwritten notes), but also visual texts (photographs, drawing, video, and actual art artifacts), spatial texts (as inscribed in landscapes and architecture), physical kinesthetic texts (an example would be dance), or other symbolically inscribed forms. Qualitative research, like quantitative research, is practiced in diverse disciplinary fields and interdisciplinary arenas, and it is applied to a vast range of social issues and problems.

### History and Context

The modern roots of qualitative research methodology can be traced from the rise of anthropology and sociology as disciplinary areas in the late 1800s and early 1900s. As is clear from Table 1.1, the emergence of these disciplines raises issues at the intersection of colonialism and industrialization.

Having its official beginnings in the colonial or industrial age, qualitative research has since evolved into a post-colonial or post-industrial state of being. The struggles that are embedded in these terms are connected to the themes, interests, and direction the methodology has taken from positivist beginnings to the more open interpretivist or constructivist perspectives of today (Denzin & Lincoln, 1994).

Table 1.1
**Historical Roots of Qualitative Research Approaches**

| Anthropology | Sociology |
|---|---|
| • Small-scale preindustrial social organization (bands, tribes, clans, kingdoms; rural, agrarian, animal husbandry)<br>• Disappearing cultures and languages<br>• Places within the realm of colonialized countries | • Large-scale evolving industrial society (bureaucracies, institutions, urban areas, industries)<br>• Emerging social problems: newsboys, office workers, management, unemployment<br>• Places within the realm of industrializing countries |

## From Research Kinds to Problem-based Research

From the beginnings of qualitative research in the late 19th century and early 20th century to the present, qualitative researchers have been deeply engaged in discussions about what I refer to as *research kinds*; that is, defining, distinguishing, and characterizing different brands of qualitative research. Each *research kind* emphasizes different approaches, perspectives, disciplinary beginnings, and other methodological characteristics. These *research kinds* have proliferated madly, creating a cluttered landscape of methodological labels and a series of ongoing arguments about which research kind should rule and why.

Qualitative *research kinds* range from ethnography, grounded theory, and case study approaches, to phenomenology, narrative analysis, and action-based research. There is also arts-based research, feminist research, and performance-based ethnography, to name just a few you might find mentioned when you peruse a qualitative research textbook.

As a qualitative researcher, I struggled to understand all the different *research kinds* and to articulate their qualities to my students. Quite frankly, however, I worried there were too many approaches described as a *research kind*, and we lacked clear distinctions among them. You only have to look at the textbooks published within the last 20 years to gauge the extent of the problem. Whereas a typical discussion of *research kinds* was once a few pages, it can now extend to multiple full chapters, and even then authors are apologetic for not accommodating all the various labeled kinds (see, e.g., Savin-Baden & Major, 2013; Patton, 2015).

I have not been the only one to notice this problem. A range of research methodologists have made calls for addressing the problem of *research kinds*; from remix (Markham, 2013), to complexity theory (Atkinson, 2005), to assemblages (Augustine, 2014) and vibrant materialism (Masny, 2013; Jackson & Mazzei, 2013); or simply interpretive dilemmas (Knoblauch, 2013), and recognition of the coexistence of multiple paradigms (Denzin, 2010).

Over time, I came to the conclusion that the different labels did not actually represent different kinds of research, but instead were used by qualitative researchers to introduce new topics for discussion within the field. So, for instance, case study research provided a means to talk about bounding studies that were not distinguished or bounded by culture (ethnography). In a similar fashion, approaches like participatory action research allowed for the introduction of new ideas about the relationship between researcher and researchee and calls for social justice as goals for research.

This insight allowed me to shift from an emphasis on describing the differences in methodological approaches to considering commonalities, which led me to develop a set of qualitative research principles that would be useful for a more generic form of qualitative research. This shift is absolutely necessary if qualitative research is going to be practiced appropriately by a diverse group of users across a broad range of disciplines, and in particular if we are to fold in those newer users working in practical arenas outside of academia.

I will refer to this generic *research kind* as *problem-based research* (Klein, 1990; Leavy, 2011). As the name says, the focus is on the problem and the best methods for addressing the problem. By taking this approach, I am emphasizing that qualitative researchers work with a shared set of common principles, although they may differ in particulars that are constantly under revision. I am also emphasizing a definition of qualitative research that is grounded in the specific kind of data and analysis with which qualitative researchers work.

## Principles of Qualitative Research

In the following section, I provide a slim overview of key principles in qualitative research that attempt to integrate the many important discussions about qualitative research methodology currently under debate. Because the characteristics of qualitative research are always in evolution, a list such as this can never be definitive nor complete. I take full responsibility for whatever shortcomings it has.

### Stance, Goals, Foundations

- The brands and strands of qualitative research are historically, philosophically, and politically diverse, but generally fall under the umbrella of an interpretivist framework.
- Qualitative researchers seek to understand the tacit or implicit issues within cultural practices and social contexts.
- The goals of qualitative research can be:
    - Descriptive (to illustrate the actions and activities found in lived experience);
    - Interpretive (to offer explanations and provide meaning related to an understanding of the lived experience);
    - Evaluative (to compare the experience to other desired outcomes or expectations);
    - Critical and/or emancipatory (to change or improve a situation); and/or
    - Theoretical (to develop broader ideas and generalizations from understanding of the experience).
- Each qualitative researcher must develop their own set of methodological principles with reference to the history of this methodology, their disciplinary focus, and the problems that they study.

### Research Design

- Qualitative research projects are bounded or focused by issues related to the problem and field, as

well as issues related to theoretical or methodological stance.
- Qualitative research studies can be located on a continuum that ranges from positivist on one end to constructivist on the other.
- Qualitative researchers are informed about the content of their studies, but they may aim to hold that knowledge aside at various points in their study as they seek to achieve an insider's understanding of the issue.
- Qualitative researchers conduct their studies in naturalized contexts or contexts that in some way allow them a form of access to understanding embedded in naturalized contexts.
- Qualitative researchers rely upon a broad range of digital tools to conduct their work—from initiation to completion.
- Team-based qualitative research, which is on the rise, brings new models and challenges to research design.

## Data

- Qualitative researchers study narrative "constructions," in the broadest possible meaning of that word, including written, visual, auditory, and spatial, among others.
- These narrative constructions are embedded in larger social discourses.
- One way to categorize forms of qualitative research data is as extant, elicited, enacted, or empowered (these terms are described later in this chapter).

## Analysis

- Analysis in qualitative research relies heavily upon the socially contextualized linguistic and cultural literacy skills (broadly defined) of the researcher.
- The researcher's embedded skills are coupled with methodological tools of contradiction (alternatively known as *research kinds*) that create alternative and challenging readings, allowing for new possibilities of understanding.

- In conducting analysis, qualitative researchers seek to decipher patterns of meaning through such techniques as close or critical reading, distillation of text through fragmentation and reconstruction, and visualization and modeling of emergent propositions.
- Qualitative researchers are attentive to presence and absence, pattern and anomaly, as they work their way through their materials.
- In qualitative research, analysis is conducted synchronously with data collection.

### Subjectivity, Ethics, Power, and Change

- In qualitative research, the researchers' subjectivity is acknowledged, affirmed, and recognized as a multifaceted and sometimes contradictory resource.
- Human social relations always contain reference to power, its exercise and implications, which is true for researchers as well as researchees.
- Qualitative researchers are ethically bound to prevent harm and recognize that this goal can only be approximated through sustained reflection and concern for those with whom they are engaged.
- Qualitative researchers work in increasingly close, mutual collaboration with the participants in a study to solve problems and advocate for change and social justice as engaged participants themselves.

### Products

- The writing up of qualitative research is a highly contested activity. The norms and expectations are in flux.
- In qualitative research, process and product are informed by the arts and humanities, not just the sciences, which can be seen in the diverse range of evolving forms by which it is presented.

## Qualitative Research Data

As I have said earlier, the kind of data qualitative researchers collect and use for their inquiries is central to the definition of this form of research. For that reason, I believe it is important early on to go into some depth to explain the things that can count as qualitative research data.

Qualitative research data come in many forms. Moreover, qualitative researchers can exercise creativity in developing new forms of materials that capture or provide information that is used to understand the questions the project is investigating. I am deeply indebted to Janet Salmons (2016), who offers a framework that provides a useful starting point for understanding the forms of qualitative research data. To her three-part description of extant, elicited, and enacted forms of data, I have added a fourth category: empowered (Table 1.2).

**Extant data** already exist. People make it for their own purposes, as opposed to creating it for the purposes of a researcher's inquiry. Extant data can be newspapers, classroom assignments, web pages, or literature. It can also be pictures hanging in an art museum or artifacts in an historical museum. It can be lurking in caves (cave paintings), on the kitchen table (shopping lists), or available on TV (TV shows or news programs).

Data that fall into the category of **Elicited** are what people most commonly think of when they hear the term "qualitative research data." Items in this category are elicited; that is, they are information requested for the purposes of learning about a defined topic. This kind of data runs the gamut from natural observations to interviews of many different sorts. Autoethnographic data, which falls into the category of elicited data, are data that the researcher creates about the topic related to their own experiences, opinions, beliefs, and persuasions (Ellis, 2004).

**Enacted** is an increasingly important form of qualitative research data. Here, researchers set a task in which participants can use their imagination or innate understanding of an issue to create a product that will provide information relevant to the inquiry. Using arts-based techniques, researchers might engage participants in drama, poetry, or visual arts to make responses that are rich with emotion and images (Leavy, 2009). Coming at it from

Table 1.2
Qualitative Research Data Framework: Adapted from Salmons' work (Salmons, 2016)

| Extant | Elicited | Enacted | Empowered |
|---|---|---|---|
| Existing materials developed "without the researcher's influence" | Constructed from participants' responses to the researcher's questions or prompts | Using "data generated with participants during the study" | Data are designed, collected, analyzed, and made sense of by researcher and researchee working together. |
| Archives<br>Published literature<br>Documents and reports<br>Databases<br>Online materials created by others<br>Unobtrusive observations | Interviews<br>Focus groups<br>Participant observation<br>Autoethnographic data, created from the researcher's self-reflection | Vignettes or problem-solving activities<br>Simulations, role plays<br>Arts-based research<br>Games | Many forms are possible from the previous three categories. However, the forms and their implementation will be shaped by participant perspectives to a much greater degree. |

a different direction, marketing researchers have been using game-based tasks to develop product information (Salmons, 2016).

I have added the category of **Empowered** to Salmon's table. Technically speaking, this is not a different kind of data, but overall a different approach to the other three forms of data. Within qualitative research, there is an ongoing strand of concern with social justice and the role, rights, and needs of those whom we study. These concerns can be seen in discussions arising about such areas as critical ethnography, participatory action research, indigenous epistemologies, and colonial/post-colonial perspectives (Dutta, 2014, Mohanty, 2003, Sanford & Angel-Ajani, 2008). As qualitative researchers, we are called to engage with participants in new ways and to make their needs our needs, and this requires that the tasks for gaining information be reshaped by collaboration.

The roles of researcher and researchee are critical tools for positioning the form of data within this framework. While some of the decisions about extant data are in the hands of the research participants—who allows the researcher access to certain documents, many of the decisions about extant data collection are solely in the hands of the researcher, who selects from publicly available data. The tasks used in elicited or enacted research are both primarily in the hands of the researcher. Empowered data shift backwards towards a more explicit and equal role for both parties.

Data-collection activities in today's digital world may be conducted in face-to-face or online/virtual environments, or a blend of the two. In an earlier time, researchers saw these as distinctly different worlds in which to practice, but today the line between the two is rapidly being erased as we move between face-to-face and online situations with increasing ease. This does not mean that there are not specific differences in planning, conducting, operating ethically, or writing up research that takes place in one environment versus another, but these differences are now seen as variations, not a dividing line (Salmons, 2016; Marres, 2017).

## Conclusion

Over the last century or more, as the world has moved through and beyond the industrial age, qualitative research has simultaneously been gaining formal methodological status and recognition as a legitimate approach for conducting social science inquiry. The road has been rocky at times, but qualitative research has held its own. The ways of learning represented by qualitative research are now widely appreciated in many disciplines and by a broad swath of research methodologists.

Qualitative research has come into its own thanks to the hearty discussions in which methodological practitioners have engaged. All aspects of the approach have been subject to rigorous arguments and debates. The issue of *research kinds* is an example of the way key discussions are constantly entering the arena for consideration.

In trying to simplify the complexity of this complicated field, this text takes the these positions:

- Qualitative research methodology is grounded in the use of qualitative research data, meaning narrative texts (of the broadest possible sort) using interpretive techniques grounded in narrative perspectives.
- Qualitative research, particularly when conducted by a complex research team, is a problem-based endeavor.
- There are common principles that can be applied to qualitative research methodology to which most researchers working with this kind of data can generally subscribe, although these principles are always in evolution and may differ from individual to individual.
- First, last, and forever in qualitative research—writing (in the broadest possible sense) is at the heart of making data, interpreting it, and sharing what we learn with others.

The recent, rapid changes in our global context ripened the world for the development of complex research teams that conduct solely qualitative or mixed-methods research. In the upcoming chapters, you will find solid, hands-on advice for ensuring your qualitative research inquiry can be conducted in a manner that will lead to the best results—good findings and interpretations—and the capacity to share this information in many forms with multiple communities around the world. You will learn about the skills you need to share your methodological, as well as your substantive, thinking. Moreover, your products will be richly written, because qualitative research, if nothing else, should be about good writing.

## References

Anders, Allison Daniel, and Jessica Nina Lester. 2015. "Lessons from Interdisciplinary Qualitative Research: Learning to Work Against a Single Story." *Qualitative Research* 15 (6): 738.

Atkinson, Paul. 2005. "Qualitative Research—Unity and Diversity." *Forum: Qualitative Social Research* 6 (3): Art 26.

Augustine, Sharon Murphy. 2014. "Living in a Post-Coding World: Analysis as Assemblage." *Qualitative Inquiry*. doi:10.1177/1077800414530258

Barone, Tom, and Elliot Eisner. 2012. *Arts Based Research*. Los Angeles, CA: Sage Publications.

Bresler, Liora, ed. 2004. *Knowing Bodies, Moving Minds: Towards Embodied Teaching and Learning*. Vol. 3, *Landscapes: The Arts, Aesthetics, and Education*. The Netherlands: Kluwer Academic Publishers.

Brocke, Jan vom, and Sonia Lippe. 2015. "Managing Collaborative Research Projects: A Synthesis of Project Management Literature and Directives for Future Research." *International Journal of Project Management* 33 (5): 1022–1039. doi:10.1016/j.ijproman.2015.02.001

Clifford, James, and George E. Marcus, eds. 1986. *Writing Culture: The Poetics and Politics of Ethnography*. Berkeley, CA: University of California Press.

Colen, Kerryn, and Roslyn Petelin. 2004. "Challenges in Collaborative Writing in the Contemporary Corporation." *Corporate Communications: An International Journal* 9 (2): 136–145. doi:10.1108/13563280410534339

Couture, B., and J. Rymer. 1989. "Interactive Writing on the Job: Definitions and Implications of 'Collaboration.'" In *Writing in the Business Professions*, edited by M. Kogan, 73–93. Urbana, IL: National Council of Teachers of English.

Curry, Leslie A., Alicia O'Cathain, Vicki L. Plano Clark, Rosalie Aroni, Michael Fetters, and David Berg. 2012. "The Role of Group Dynamics in Mixed Methods Health Sciences Research Teams." *Journal of Mixed Methods Research* 6 (1): 5.

Davidson, Judith. 2004. "Embodied Knowledge: Possibilities and Constraints in Arts Education and Curriculum." In *Knowing Bodies, Moving Minds: Towards Embodied Teaching and Learning*, edited by Liora Bresler, 197–212. The Netherlands: Kluwer Academic Publishers.

Davidson, Judith, and Silvana di Gregorio. 2011. "Qualitative Research and Technology: In the Midst of a Revolution." In *The Sage Handbook of Qualitative Research*, edited by Norman K. Denzin and Yvonna S. Lincoln, 627–643. Los Angeles, CA: Sage Publications.

Davidson, Judith, Trena Paulus, and Kristi Jackson. 2016. "Speculating on the Future of Digital Tools for Qualitative Research." *Qualitative Inquiry* (7): 606.

Denzin, Norman K. 2003. *Performance Ethnography: Critical Pedagogy and the Politics of Culture*. Thousand Oaks, CA: Sage Publications.

Denzin, Norman K. 2010. "Moments, Mixed Methods, and Paradigm Dialogs." *Qualitative Inquiry* 16 (6): 419–427. doi:10.1177/1077800410364608

Denzin, Norman K., and Yvonna S. Lincoln, eds. 1994. *Handbook of Qualitative Research*. Thousand Oaks, CA.

di Gregorio, Silvana, and Judith Davidson. 2008. *Qualitative Research Design for Software Users*: Maidenhead, Berkshire: Open University Press, 2008.

Döös, Marianne, and Lena Wilhelmson. 2014. "Proximity and Distance: Phases of Intersubjective Qualitative Data Analysis in a Research Team." *Quality & Quantity: International Journal of Methodology* 48 (2): 1089–1106. doi:10.1007/s11135-012-9816-y

Drouin, Nathalie, and Mario Bourgault. 2013. "How Organizations Support Distributed Project Teams." *Journal of Management Development* 32 (8): 865–885. doi:10.1108/jmd-07-2012-0091

Dutta, Urmitapa. 2014 "Critical Ethnography." In *Qualitative Methodologies: A Practical Guide*, edited by Jane Mills and Melanie Birks, 89–105. London: Sage Publications.

Dutta, Urmitapa. 2016. "Ethnographic Approaches." In *Handbook of Methodological Approaches to Community-based Research: Qualitative, Quantitative, and Mixed Methods*, edited by Leonard Jason and David Glenwick, 69–79. Oxford, UK: Oxford University Press.
Ede, L. S., and A. Lunsford. 1990. *Singular Texts/Plural Authors: Perspectives on Collaborative Writing*. Carbondale, IL: Southern Illinois Press.
Ellis, Carolyn. 2004. *The ethnographic I: A methodological novel about autoethnography*. Walnut Creek, CA: AltaMira Press.
Ely, M., R. Vinz, M. Anzul, and M. Downing. 1997. *On Writing Qualitative Research: Living by Words*. London: The Falmer Press.
Faulkner, Sandra. 2009. *Poetry as Method: Reporting Research Through Verse*. Walnut, Creek, CA: Left Coast Press.
Foster, J. W., F. Chiang, R. I. Burgos, R. E. Cáceres, C. M. Tejada, A. T. Almonte, F. R. Noboa, L. J. Perez, M. F. Urbaez, and A. Heath. 2012. "Community-based Participatory Research and the Challenges of Qualitative Analysis Enacted by Lay, Nurse, and Academic Researchers." *Research in Nursing & Health* 35 (5): 550–559. 10p. doi:10.1002/nur.21494
Geertz, Clifford. 1973. *The Interpretation of Cultures: Selected Essays by Clifford Geertz*. New York: Basic Books.
Gershon, Walter, ed. 2009. *The Collaborative Turn: Working Together in Qualitative Research*. Rotterdam, The Netherlands: Sense Publications.
Gerstl-Pepin, Cynthia I., and Michael G. Gunzenhauser. 2002. "Collaborative Team Ethnography and the Paradoxes of Interpretation." *International Journal of Qualitative Studies in Education (QSE)* 15 (2): 137.
"Globalization." 2016. Wikipedia. https://en.wikipedia.org/wiki/Globalization.
Haythornthwaite, Caroline. 2006. "Learning and Knowledge Networks in Interdisciplinary Collaborations." *Journal of the American Society for Information Science and Technology* 57 (8): 1079–1092. doi:10.1002/asi.20371
Hesse-Biber, Sharlene. 2015. "Introduction: Navigating a Turbulent Research Landscape: Working the Boundaries, Tensions, Diversity, and Contradictions of Multimethod and Mixed Methods Inquiry." In *The Oxford Handbook of Multimethod and Mixed Methods Research Inquiry*, edited by Sharlene Hesse-Biber and R. Burke Johnson, xxxiii–liii. Oxford, UK: Oxford University Press.
Hesse-Biber, Sharlene, Deborah Rodriguez, and Nollaig A. Frost. 2015. "A Qualitatively Driven Approach to Multimethod and Mixed Methods Research." In *The Oxford Handbook of Multimethod and Mixed Methods Research Inquiry*, edited by Sharlene Hesse-Biber and R. Burke Johnson, 3–20. Oxford, UK: Oxford University Press.
Jackson, Alecia Y., and A. Lisa Mazzei. 2013. "Plugging One Text into Another: Thinking with Theory in Qualitative Research." *Qualitative Inquiry* 19 (4): 261–271. doi:10.1177/1077800412471510
Jarzabkowski, Paula, Rebecca Bednarek, and Laure Cabantous. 2015. "Conducting Global Team-based Ethnography: Methodological Challenges and Practical Methods." *Human Relations* 68 (1): 3.
Kinzie, Jillian, Peter Magolda, Adrianna Kezar, George Kuh, Sara Hinkle, and Elizabeth Whitt. 2007. "Methodological Challenges in Multi-Investigator

Multi-Institutional Research in Higher Education." *Higher Education* 54 (3): 469–482. doi:10.1007/s10734-006-9007-7

Klein, Julie. 1990. *Interdisciplinary Approach to Knowledge*. Detroit, MI: Wayne State University Press.

Knoblauch, Hubert. 2013. "Qualitative Methods at the Crossroads: Recent Developments in Interpretive Social Research." *Forum: Qualitative Social Research* 14 (3): Art. 12.

Knowles, J. Gary, and Ardra L. Cole, eds. 2008. *Handbook of the Arts in Qualitative Research*. Thousand Oaks, CA: Sage Publications.

Lather, Patti. 2013. "Methodology-21: What Do We Do in the Afterward?" *International Journal of Qualitative Studies in Education (QSE)* 26 (6): 634–645. doi:10.1080/09518398.2013.788753

Lather, Patti, and Elizabeth A. St. Pierre. 2013. "Post-qualitative Research." *International Journal of Qualitative Studies in Education* 26 (6): 629–633. doi:10.1080/09518398.2013.788752

Leavy, Patricia. 2009. *Method Meets Art: Arts-Based Research Practice*. New York: The Guilford Press.

Leavy, Patricia. 2011. *Essentials of Transdisciplinary Research: Using Problem-centered Methodologies*. Walnut Creek, CA: Left Coast Press.

LeFevre, Karen Burke. 1987. *Invention as a Social Act*. Carbondale, IL: Southern Illinois University Press.

Liggett, Annette M., Corrine E. Glesne, A. P. Johnston, Susan Brody Hasazi, and Richard A. Schattman. 1994. "Teaming in Qualitative Research: Lessons Learned." *International Journal of Qualitative Studies in Education (QSE)* 7 (1): 77.

Lowry, Paul Benjamin, Aaron Curtis, and Michelle Rene Lowry. 2004. "Building a Taxonomy and Nomenclature of Collaborative Writing to Improve Interdisciplinary Research and Practice." *Journal of Business Communication* 41: 66–99.

Markham, Annette N. 2013. "Remix Cultures, Remix Methods: Reframing Qualitative Inquiry for Social Media Contexts." In *Global Dimensions of Qualitative Inquiry*, edited by Norman K. Denzin and Michael D. Giardina, 63–81. Walnut Park, CA: Left Coast Press.

Marres, Noortje. 2017. *Digital Sociology: The Reinvention of Social Research*. Cambridge, UK: Polity Press.

Masny, Diana. 2013. "Rhizoanalytic Pathways in Qualitative Research." *Qualitative Inquiry* 19 (5): 339.

Mauthner, Natasha S., and Andrea Doucet. 2008. "'Knowledge Once Divided Can Be Hard to Put Together Again': An Epistemological Critique of Collaborative and Team-Based Research Practices." *Sociology* 42 (5): 971.

Mohanty, Chandra Talpade. 2003. *Feminism Without Borders: Decolonizing Theory, Practicing Solidarity*. Durham, NC: Duke University Press.

Palmeri, Jason. 2004. "When Discourses Collide: A Case Study of Interprofessional Collaborative Writing in a Medically Oriented Law Firm." *International Journal of Business Communication* 41 (1): 37–65.

Patton, Michael. 2015. *Qualitative Research and Evaluation Methods: Integrating Theory and Practice*. 4th ed. Los Angeles: Sage Publications.

Paulus, Trena, Jessica Nina Lester, and Paul G. Dempster. 2014. *Digital Tools for Qualitative Research*. Thousand Oaks, CA: Sage.

Paulus, Trena, Marianne Woodside, and Mary Ziegler. 2008. "Extending the Conversation: Qualitative Research as Dialogic Collaborative Process." *The Qualitative Report* (2): 226.

St. Pierre, Elizabeth Adams. 2012. "Another Postmodern Report on Knowledge: Positivism and Its Others." *International Journal of Leadership in Education* 15 (4): 483.

St. Pierre, Elizabeth Adams. 2014. "A Brief and Personal History of Post Qualitative Research Toward 'Post Inquiry.'" *JCT: Journal of Curriculum Theorizing* 30 (2): 2-19.

Punch, K., and A. Oancea. 2014. *Introduction to Research Methods in Education*. 2nd ed. Los Angeles: Sage Publications.

Repko, Allen, and Rick Szostak. 2017. *Interdisciplinary Research: Process and Theory*. Los Angeles, CA: Sage Publications.

Richardson, Laurel. 1994. "Writing: A Method of Inquiry." In *The Sage Handbook of Qualitative Research*, edited by Norman K. Denzin and Yvonna S. Lincoln, 516-529. Thousand Oaks, CA: Sage Publications.

Ricketts, Edward Flanders, and Jack Calvin. 1968. *Between Pacific Tides [by] Edward F. Ricketts and Jack Calvin*. Stanford, CA: Stanford University Press.

Rogers-Dillon, Robin H. 2005. "Hierarchical Qualitative Research Teams: Refining the Methodology." *Qualitative Research* 5 (4): 437-454. doi:10.1177/1468794105056922

Salmons, Janet. 2016. *Doing Qualitative Research Online*. Los Angeles, CA: Sage Publications.

Sanford, Victoria, and Asale Angel-Ajani, eds. 2006. *Engaged Observer: Anthropology, Advocacy, and Activism*. New Brunswick, NJ: Rutgers University Press.

Savin-Baden, M., and Claire Howell Major. 2013. *Qualitative Research: The Essential Guide to Theory and Practice*. New York: Routledge.

Siemens, Lynne, Liu Yin, and Jefferson Smith. 2014. "Mapping Disciplinary Differences and Equity of Academic Control to Create a Space for Collaboration." *Canadian Journal of Higher Education* 44 (2): 49-67.

"Social Fictions Series." 2017. Sense Publishers, last modified 7/24/2017. https://www.sensepublishers.com/catalogs/bookseries/social-fictions-series/.

Taylor, Carol A., and Gabrielle Ivinson. 2013. "Material Feminisms: New Directions for Education." *Gender & Education* 25 (6): 665-670. doi:10.1080/09540253.2013.834617

Van Steendam, E. 2016. "Editorial: Forms of Collaboration In Writing." *Journal of Writing Research* 8 (2): 183-204. doi:10.17239/jowr-2016.08.02.01

Wasser, Judith Davidson, and Liora Bresler. 1996. "Working in the Interpretive Zone: Conceptualizing Collaboration in Qualitative Research Teams." *Educational Researcher* 25 (5): 5-15.

Wolf, Margery. 1992. *A Thrice-Told Tale: Feminism, Postmodernism, and Ethnographic Responsibility*. Stanford, CA: Stanford University Press.

"Why We Post." 2016. https://www.ucl.ac.uk/why-we-post.

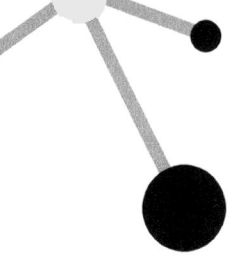

# RESEARCH DESIGN IN TEAM-BASED QUALITATIVE RESEARCH

**Qualitative Research Begins in Writing**

Writing—or composing, to think of it more broadly—is central to the work of qualitative researchers, from the beginning of a project with the research design, to its completion in products that share the knowledge and ideas created from the study. Through the quality of the design, you lay the foundation for your thinking, and, thus, your writing. This research design work is conducted through talking, writing, and thinking round and round in circles with yourself and the others working with you on an inquiry.

Many researchers, beginners in particular, may be more focused on the data collection or results that come later in the project and do not realize design work is highly imaginative and equally interesting. Good research design requires imagination; a "what if" form of thinking. You have to use your mind's eye and make your best guess. Your imaginative work will be grounded in experience—gleaned practically from work on other pieces of research or from other experienced members of the team. It will also be informed through the writings of others who have worked in this form of methodology, grappled with this particular topic, or travelled in this part of the world. In the end, however, it will be your best guess.

In this chapter, I discuss three critical components of research design that are reliant on writing and establish the foundation for the future writing up of the research. Without attention to these three issues, methodological and substantive writing possibilities will be confounded, and the project will have difficulty moving forward:

- Team formation
- Research design and project organization
- Caring: internalized and externalized

There is much writing required in the research design and initiation phase of a project. Although this writing may not end up in a peer-reviewed journal or other dissemination channel, it establishes the foundation for all other writing in the project, pointing the way and creating the shape of what will come. This unpublished writing should not be deemed trivial or ephemeral. In team-based qualitative research, preliminary writing is an opportunity to both develop shared understanding and trust, as well as document key decisions that will guide future project work for all team members. Initial writing forms the basis for a research team to build trust, create structures, decipher weak points, and improve processes.

## Team Formation

### Principles: Teams and Qualitative Research

There are various roles qualitative research can play in the overall research design of a project, just as there are diverse roles qualitative researchers can play on a research team. For instance, some teams will only use qualitative research methods; other teams will move back and forth between qualitative and other methods; still other teams might have a separate group just to conduct the qualitative research component, which will report its results but not participate otherwise with other members of the team. The possibilities for mixing qualitative research within a team are many (Hesse-Biber, Rodriguez, & Frost, 2015).

Having said that, by following the principles stated next, a complex qualitative research team will do much to ensure the integrity of their project results:

- All team members, regardless of their area of expertise, are informed about qualitative research and how it will contribute to the project;
- Qualitative research components of the project are designed in a manner consistent with qualitative research principles (see Chapter 1);
- There is adequate qualitative research expertise on the team, or available to it, to insure that qualitative research principles can be upheld, understood, and translated to team members and others as needed; and,
- Qualitative research principles are reflected upon in interpretive meetings and during the development of results and writing up of the research.

Some research teams planning to undertake qualitative research will possess an abundance of knowledge and skills in the area of qualitative research, but others will not. There are many experts and consultants available now who can assist in the design, conduct, and completion of the qualitative research components of a project. If you don't possess these skills, but need them, connect with people who do, just as one does with survey or statistical approaches.

## Gathering the Group

Teams are formed in many ways, from colleagues with offices across the hall who speak to each other frequently, to academics and nonprofit leaders who meet at the talk of a speaker presenting on a topic of interest. Colleagues can be found at professional conferences bringing together people with interest on a shared topic. Sometimes teams are formed by an individual's reputation. In these cases, members may not personally know each other in advance, but they want to address a particular need or submit a proposal that needs certain expertise, a kind of e-Harmony or blind date approach for project formation. Professional colleagues may make introductions to bring researchers together for a joint project. "How we met" can be as interesting a topic for researchers to narrate as it is for romantic partners and married couples!

Through analysis of 1,103 interdisciplinary grant proposals submitted to the National Science Foundation over a period of three years, one study examined the ways interdisciplinary teams come together (Lungeanu, Huang, & Contractor, 2014). The researchers found that, among academic proposal submitters, there was a rich combination of variables at play in the formation of such teams. Of importance, the desire to engage in such collaborations had much to do with the ways individuals were embedded in professional networks, and, interestingly, women were found to be more likely to engage in collaboration.

Business literature has made interesting contributions to our understanding of team roles. For instance, in looking at virtually and physically far-flung collaborative groups, Eubanks et al. (2016) realized that traditional leadership patterns had fragmented. Successful team groupings in these new circumstances needed to include people who were task-oriented and could translate ideas into action. In line with their findings, a study of virtual teams in a European computer producer demonstrated that traditional models of team functioning were too linear in form. To truly understand how modern teams function required a more dynamic, flattened, and fluid model (Buhlman, 2006).

## Role of Qualitative Research on the Team

On a complex research team, qualitative research occupies one of two positions:

> *Solely qualitative research teams:* On a solely qualitative research team, there may be some limited use of descriptive statistics, but overall the only forms of data collected and analyzed are qualitative in nature. In other words, numbers are used sparingly, and texts are approached in an interpretive manner.
> 
> *Mixed methods teams:* On mixed methods teams, a mixture of quantitative and qualitative data is collected. The sequence, organization, and use of these two forms of data will vary from team to team, depending on the project and its research design (Hesse-Biber, Rodriguez, & Frost, 2015)

These positions or designations may not be continuous across a complex study. In a mixed methods study, there may be synchronous or asynchronous use of one or the other form, and even in a solely qualitative research study, there may be multiple staged uses of different forms of qualitative research (Hesse-Biber, Rodriguez, & Frost, 2015).

The process of team formation and the role allocated to qualitative research during that process will say much about the way the project will unfold and the contribution qualitative research will be able to make the knowledge of the project. Using mixed methods research teams as their starting point, Curry et al. (2012) illustrate how team members function as representational groups in which multiple forms of identities (methodological, disciplinary, and others) are in play.

For these reasons, it will be important for members to probe their assumptions about qualitative research and the role it will play in this particular project. For instance, will qualitative research be foregrounded or backgrounded? Will qualitative research data be used to affirm quantitative findings, or will qualitative research be used to search for unique findings?

## Difference as Attribute

The role of qualitative research on the team is only one of the variables of difference of which teams are composed. Teams may also vary in regard to location and dispersion of team members. For instance, all team members can be located in the same geographic location, at many sites with a central hub site, or at diverse sites with no central site. Geographical diversity suggests they could be located within the same or different institutions, perhaps within the same state or national jurisdictions, but they may also be operating across regional, national, or international boundaries that can raise significant financial, planning, and legal problems (Garland et al., 2006; Buhlman, 2006). Buhlman (2006), among others, devotes considerable space to exploring the definition and characteristics of virtual teams, emphasizing the importance of touch (regular communication) and trust (the belief that all team members have each other's back) as crucial features to pay attention to in the initial phases of team formation.

Team variation is also present in the internal organization of the team, where levels of distinction, status, or hierarchies can run the gamut from highly stratified to highly communal, and everything in between. Some of the differences will be disciplinary or methodologically based, and some will be personal preferences of the team members. Other differences that may be present include: gender, race, culture, ethnicity, language, sexual orientation, religious preference, or political leanings, to name just a few.

Another issue of difference that will be significant is the role or stance toward research that is held by each team member. Depending on training and inclination, some team members may regard themselves as observers, others as participants, and still others as actors for change. Mauthner and Doucet (2008, p. 971) discuss the tension that exists within teams among members employing qualitative research theories that are grounded in a "postfoundational epistemological paradigm" and members who subscribe to "normative team-based research practices [that] embody foundational principles." They argue for paying careful attention to reflexive practices to ensure the knowledge of all members of a team will be honored. Resisting the division-of-labor model, which characterizes many research teams, they call for a relations of labor model.

Regardless of the model that is used within a team, it will be critical to ensure these roles and their tasks are integrated; that there are adequate checks, oversight, and training; and that the materials and their analysis are thoughtfully organized. All of this requires a lot of pre-thinking, thinking in process, and post-reflection to make sure the work proceeds efficiently and with integrity. Bringing it all together across time and space can be very complicated. Ultimately, you want good, trustworthy results, depending on what you and others mean by that, and while teams can make some things easier . . . they can also make some things harder.

The more humans you add, the more complex the work becomes, and the more important it is to spend time developing the groundwork. Garland et al. (2006) suggest that one should always assume team research will be more time-consuming than individual research, and, moreover, qualitative research conducted in a team setting will take significantly more time.

Teams bring complexity, no matter what the process of formation, level of prior knowledge, or other issues. Complex qualitative research teams will be most successful if members devote sufficient time and effort to getting to know each other, their perspectives and strengths from a disciplinary and methodological perspective, as well as in regard to other areas of difference. Acknowledging diversity and establishing trust are critical if a team is going to be successful on a project (Curry et al., 2012; Creamer, 2003).

## Developing a Negotiation and Dissemination Agreement

I strongly urge that this piece of work be tackled very early in the planning stages of a project. Unfortunately, many teams deal with this component when they encounter it as a problem, and it may already be too late to develop an amicable decision. If you want to avoid massive headaches, make this agreement one of your first tasks, returning to it over time as needed.

### Negotiation Component

Ultimately, whether it is formal and written, or informal and simply agreed upon—a team needs a charter that describes its fundamental principles, including how members will work together and negotiate differences and statuses. As you approach this task:

- Do not assume everyone is working on the same set of principles.
- Do not assume communication about these issues has been transparent to all.
- Do not assume everyone is speaking their mind openly.

Create a safe space in which to explore each member's assumptions, and be committed to digging down deep to uncover differences, concerns, and potential misunderstandings. Ironically, doing this thing that can seem so hard will build trust that will translate into a better working process.

You can assume your charter (in whatever form) will be continually revised as you come to know each other better and have research experiences together. As Garland et al. (2006, p. 105) note, "Document these expectations for accountability in a written contract. Renegotiate that contract as the parameters of the project change (as they will)."

*Dissemination Component*

Dissemination is a responsibility for all research projects, regardless of the organization in which they are lodged. Dissemination can lead to the solving of important social problems as well as bringing fame, recognition, and more resources to one's work, but it also entails risks and responsibilities, both internal and external, to project members. In team-based research, the good news is that there are more hands to lighten the load; the bad news is that more hands make for more negotiation about dissemination. "Develop a written policy for authorship of all publications from the project, reviewing those of other projects and recognizing that the policy will need to be reviewed periodically" (Garland et al., 2006, p. 106). Such a policy will not only protect team members from making ethical violations, it will also lessen tension through increasing transparency around publication expectations.

At the very least, a dissemination agreement should document decisions about these issues:

- Who "owns" the data?
- If the project is grant-supported, does the funder have dissemination requirements that need to be followed?
- Who are the critical gatekeepers in regard to making decisions about the use of the data or public discussion of the project?
- What are the rights or responsibilities of different project roles in regard to data use or public discussion of the project?
- What is the process for a project member to follow when s/he would like to use the data for a writing or dissemination project?
- Who should review documents, materials, or other dissemination items to ensure that the guidelines have been followed?

An important rule for any team member to follow in regard to making use of project data and/or speaking publicly for a project is to consult with the team leadership if there are any questions or ambiguities about how an issue should be handled.

## Research Design and Project Organization

There are several important decision-making areas team leaders need to consider as they begin to sketch out plans for the project. These decision-making areas will have far reaching implications for the writing up of the project. These include:

- Establishing expectations for preliminary and ongoing documentation of team activity;
- Selecting methods of inquiry;
- Initiating a project management system using a digital toolkit approach; and,
- Integrating research design with a long-term data archiving plan.

### Establishing Expectations for Preliminary and Ongoing Documentation of Team Activity

Documentation begins at the initiation of the project and is continuous, ongoing, and synchronous with the unfolding of the project. Documenting who the team is, how it came together, and what early decisions were made in regard to team functioning, is an important part of a qualitative research methodological description (Wasser & Bresler, 1996).

This early methodological writing becomes the core of key project documents: a research proposal and/or funding proposal, a submission to some form of institutional review board (IRB) for ethical clearance, and materials that will be foundational to approaching sites and participants.

Who will document what and when, how the documentation will be stored, and how it can be accessed are all decisions that the team will need to grapple with early on in the process. Notes from meetings, a repository for email in which decisions are noted, memos written by team members, and unpublished papers or literature reviews written as the project gets underway—all of these may be important to telling the story of the project and describing how it came to its ultimate conclusions.

Regardless of the kind of research one plans to undertake—quantitative or qualitative—many people underestimate the time and commitment required to design robust research. The larger the team involved in the planning of a research project, the more time will be required to bring people together, solidify viewpoints, and develop shared goals and language. Time to do these tasks is critical if the project is going to get off to the right start.

While the substantive topic of inquiry may be well understood by group members, they will still need to explore the important questions grounding the proposal: What do we want to know about this topic? How can we learn about it? How will the documentation be collected? What tools for inquiry should we select? Again, documenting discussions about these issues is important to understand the principles of the proposal you will be submitting and recall key concerns of different team members.

### Selecting Methods of Inquiry

Once decisions about the inquiry forms have been made by the team, assignments can be given to search for extant materials or develop protocols or instructions for other forms of data collection, such as interviews, observations, or visual data construction. These tasks are critical to preparing for submission to an oversight ethical body, as well as planning for and developing the data management system for the project. Thus, writing about, for, and around methods of inquiry becomes an important early form of writing up the research.

Developing the materials that will be used for the data tasks helps the research team to imagine what will be coming and how to prepare for the different possibilities. For instance, creating interview protocols will not only include developing questions to be asked of others, but also describing the procedures around the interview—from instructions to participants to checklists for equipment to have on hand. This helps researchers think through what must be done prior to, during, and after the actual interview. Thus, what may appear to be a mundane task to some, such as writing up step-by-step instructions, is, in the larger scheme of things, actually very imaginative. By doing this kind of pre-planning well, complex teams will be able to function more efficiently down the line.

An added benefit to the hard labor of writing out data-collection instructions is that once a set of procedures is worked out, they are like moveable knowledge objects that can be repurposed and plopped down into other projects with similar tasks and requirements. In the project on views of teen sexting in which I served as the primary qualitative research authority, I developed directions for the focus group interviewing process that have subsequently been used by myself and others in a variety of projects (Harris et al., 2013). An example of these materials can be found in the Appendices A and B.

In thinking about what forms of inquiry will be used, particularly for a large team, it is essential that one think about—how much will be collected. The larger the team, the more pressure there will be to collect large amounts of data. In addition, qualitative researchers, working on a team with other members more grounded in quantitative perspectives, may compromise by agreeing to collect more qualitative data than makes sense in order to satisfy fears that without a larger sample, the qualitative component won't be seen as trustworthy. In a qualitative research study, however, too much data can be too much of a good thing. The promise of qualitative research is to go deep and look at the complexity of ideas and situations that cannot yet be reduced to variables. Going deep takes good data collected in places where there is an expectation for learning. Team leadership needs to ensure the qualitative research data collected will be able to serve the possibilities qualitative research methods can bring to the project. When it comes to how much qualitative research data you should collect, I often say to students, "A little can go a long way," or "Less is more."

## Initiating a Project Management System Using a Digital Toolkit Approach

It is the sad truth that discussions of databases, document organization, or filing systems have garnered little useful attention among qualitative researchers. For many qualitative researchers, the very term—database—strikes a discordant note in their hearts, suggesting large sample sizes, quantitative approaches, and unfamiliar research discourse. Such terms are not "QR" in their eyes, meaning humanistic or interpretive.

Interestingly, gender issues may also count here. Men may feel paying attention to these small details to be feminine in nature, and thus may not care to address these issues. Women, however, may disregard them because they feel attending to them would mark them as stereotypically feminine.

Regardless of why this happens, failure to attend to how project materials are organized and made available, especially when working with complex teams, can lead to real frustration, and, even worse, a project that never gets analyzed and results that will never be shared or disseminated. Suffice it to say that in qualitative research, as in all research, you will stand or fall by your system of organization. This is true for individual researchers . . . and even truer for qualitative research teams.

While every complex research team is different, there are also many similarities across groups. This means there will be a sharp learning curve with your first experience, but, thankfully, in subsequent experiences with team research, you will have much to draw upon, from knowledge of processes and systems, to information about tools and their functioning.

Building an organizational system to support the multiple needs of a complex team requires careful discussions that reach deep into the future of the project. Attention must be paid to the amount and kind of data that will be collected, as well as the processes of incorporating new items into the system, raising such questions as: How should materials be labeled? How should they be submitted? To whom? How will the materials be processed? How will team members have access to the corpus? How will secondary materials like memos be integrated? How will research literature be integrated? These questions and many, many more like them will be answered as you build the organizational system to support the project.

### *Digital Toolkit Approach*

In a digital world, we are dependent on digital tools for all facets of research work, from research design and data collection to analysis and writing. Selecting the digital tools project members will use and providing opportunities for all members to become familiar with their use is a critical part of the research design phase as the project gets underway. A toolkit approach is a good way to conceptualize what is needed because it supports the research team to think across the many kinds of tasks they will be undertaking and to give serious consideration to integration and efficiencies (Paulus, Lester, & Dempster, 2014). What I present next is a blend of thinking regarding the digital toolkit required for a qualitative researcher and the digital toolkit required for complex qualitative team operation. It is up to each team to shape a toolkit that meets the methodological needs of a given project. Mixed methods projects will, necessarily, include tools that will allow the organizing and managing of quantitative data in addition to qualitative data. That being said, integration of the systems should also be considered.

In developing a digital toolkit for project organization, it is important to remember that the internet and digital tools are constantly changing and being redeveloped. The tools that may be perfect at the initiation of a project may need tweaking along the way as circumstances change and new opportunities arise. Because of the time and expense of assembling and operating a complex research team, the projects undertaken tend to be long and fairly complicated. Multi-year projects may well need to adopt different iterations of the digital tools they are using over the span of their work.

For this reason, it is important to think about the functions one needs, more than a particular brand of tool. For instance, the need for a collaborative writing tool could be served by Microsoft Word on one team and Google Docs on another team. Likewise, one team may be using NVivo for their QDAS tool, another Dedoose, and yet another Quirkos—it depends on the members' skills, their access to the specific tool, and the needs of the project. In advocating for a digital toolkit, I am not trying to sell any particular software or hardware. One of the few things I can be certain of is that all digital tools in use today will change over time (Table 2.1).

## Communication and Project Management

On a complex team, there is a range of tools that undergird the organization of the work.

*Synchronous and Asynchronous Communication Tools for Individual and Group Interactions* In a digital world, all team members will need access to synchronous communication tools (smartphone, chat,

Table 2.1

**Components of the Digital Toolkit (Emphasis on Qualitative Research)**

| Communication and Project Management | Data and Literature Collection | Qualitative Research Data Organization and Management |
|---|---|---|
| -Synchronous and asynchronous communication tools for individual and group interactions<br>-Project planning tools<br>-Digital storage<br>-Tools to support individual and collaborative writing<br>-Dissemination tools including social media forms | *Data Collection*: Will vary based upon face-to-face or virtual collection of data. Might include audio and visual recording, mobile applications, and note-taking devices.<br><br>*Literature Collection:*<br>-Reference Manager<br>-Web clipping and note taking | -Qualitative Data Analysis Software (QDAS): necessary for organizing materials collected from diverse members in diverse forms and analyzed by a broad number of individuals. Provides tools for organization, visualization, and probing materials. Be aware of how the tool allows for (or restricts) collaboration.<br>-Tool selected should integrate with Reference Manager, note-taking, and other digital tools used in project. |

etc.) and asynchronous communication tools (email, attachments, and voice mail). Even when sitting back-to-back in the same office, today's workers communicate digitally a large portion of the time. Depending on the form of the project, these tools should be tested to work across diverse institutional, geographical, and national settings with efficiency and ease, supporting whatever idiosyncrasies may be part of this particular team's communication issues. While this may seem like stating the obvious in a globalizing and digitalizing world, in truth there are still significant contrasts in digital use across disciplinary, institutional, national, and other boundaries. Probe the differences and early on figure out the possibilities and challenges for communications.

*Project Planning Tools (Initial Planning and Ongoing)* From Gantt charts and Excel spreadsheets to Kanban boards and many other forms of software and applications, project-planning tools abound in today's world. In complex projects with many interacting parts and players, these tools can be invaluable in tracking what is being done, who is doing what, and how much is left to do. While much project planning and tracking can be done without specialized software, new tools are emerging that help team members to visualize project tasks and easily understand the progress of different parts.

*Digital Storage* The days of research offices clogged with five-drawer metal filing cabinets storing vast amounts of paper notes is just about over. I still have a couple myself, but it's only because my career started in the pre-digital age! Most of us are now operating in a world where digital storage rules. The larger the project, the more storage a team will need; the more sensitive the topic, the more security that digital storage will require; the larger the team, the more rules about organizing the storage will be needed. It is a bureaucracy in the making.

Once upon a time, storage security was a simple proposition—make sure the filing cabinet was under lock and key—but today it is much more complicated. Where are the servers located? What kind of security protocol is followed? What kind of back-up services are there? What happens if there is a security breach—will participants be harmed? Some projects will work with server space provided by their institution(s); others will locate materials in commercial storage providers like Dropbox or OneDrive. The IRB overseeing the project's ethical decisions are likely to have certain requirements regarding location and security of data.

*Tools to Support Individual and Collaborative Writing* Word processing has come a long way in the short history of modern computer software. It's hard to remember that not too long ago, we typed on manual typewriters, with carbons, erasing our errors with stuff called "White-out," that handy little white paint that covered up the type, and before that we used pencils and fountain pens! Today's word processors, from MS Word to Google Docs, are not only places to enter written text, but they also provide many visualization tools, allowing us to think with text in new ways. We can review others' work and track changes with bright colors; we can use headers that create an outline in the navigation pane; and we can insert a variety of comments on digital Post-Its, in thought bubbles, or in audiovisual form. Moreover, there are new forms of software emerging specifically designed to be used for writing, such as the widely touted Scrivener. Many unexpected kinds of writing tasks can emerge during the course of a project, and it is useful to have several tools up your sleeve, so to speak, that can get you through a variety of tasks in an efficient manner.

*Dissemination Tools, Including Social Media Forms* Project dissemination begins with project initiation. This may come in the form of a press release from your institution or the creation of a website for information announcing your project to the world. Dissemination is an opportunity and a challenge, but it is always with you and never goes away. Most hardcore researchers have been trained to focus exclusively on research and only turn to these tasks after the completion of all other project tasks. I strongly urge you not to do this, but to develop the dissemination component of your digital toolkit early on and to make a staged plan for sharing out information about the project as it moves forward. Project products can come at many places in the work—from a meta-review of research literature on the topic, to a paper reporting on preliminary results from the first round of data collected, or a methodological paper describing an issue related to developing a digital toolkit for the team. Many researchers focus exclusively on publication in peer-reviewed journals with competitive impact factors, but there is also a range of other opportunities to share information on the work that prime the pump for information on your work. Twitter, Facebook, blogs, and other digital media should be included in the dissemination plan—or whatever new form of social media is in operation in the future.

## Data and Literature Collection

Each project will curate a unique collection of data and literature based upon factors selective to that project, from the topic under study, to the disciplines involved in the work.

*Data Collection* Data collection will vary, based upon multiple factors, including the kind of data to be collected, whether it is collected face-to-face or virtually, issues of confidentiality, access to technologies, and even, in some locations—access to electricity and/or the internet. Chapter 1 of this book provides a definition of qualitative research data and a framework for understanding the forms of data that constitute qualitative research data.

The tools needed to collect diverse forms of qualitative research also vary widely. Today, mobile, digital devices are favored. Cell phones and tablets alone can do almost everything that used to be assigned to separate tools like audio or visual recording equipment. Data collected virtually might also come from email or Facebook threads. There are tools to collect hybrid forms of data, such as Lecture Capture in which a PowerPoint presentation and an audiovisual recording of a presentation are combined to allow those not present to have the full experience of a live presentation. Web pages and online artifacts may be captured by a Notes tool or Reference Manager. Digital developments are very fluid in this area and will require monitoring to make the best choices for each team.

*Literature Collection* In the last few decades, the amount of extant information—meaning stuff that is out there created by others, professional or not—that we must process as individuals in daily life is overwhelming. This exploding trend is particularly daunting for those who are considered to be knowledge workers—such as social science researchers. There are more journals of every sort, which means many more articles on topics related to our focus. While peer-reviewed materials are critical to understanding academic knowledge, researchers must also make sense of popular materials on their topics, which often indicate critical new directions for their field. It is for these reasons that individual researchers and team-based researchers must rely upon reference-management tools, in conjunction with other digital tools, such as note-taking tools, if they are to have any hope of surviving the onslaught (Lubke et al., 2017).

*Reference Managers* Reference Managers come in many sizes, shapes, and forms. I am currently using Endnote because my university provides a site license, but I have also used Mendeley and Zotero, and there are many other forms of these useful and important tools, from RefWorks to Paper. Again, one certainty in life is that these tools, too, shall change over time as new ones are made available.

For teams making use of a Reference Manager, it will be important to set up procedures for literature collection and processing. Team members should have training on how to share their literature and work in team libraries. A team will need to decide when and how to rely on the Reference Manager and when to shift materials into QDAS for a closer or fine-grained reading. The better the team is trained in the use of these tools, the more efficiently the team will be able to move into writing mode.

Developing and enriching the literature database and discussion of its contents should be an ongoing part of the project work. Limiting connection to the literature review and reference manager to the lowest level of project worker and the smallest amount of project talk time is not a good strategy. Literature database work is creative work, and, moreover, it is a gift that keeps on giving long into the future for all members of the project. The collections of materials you curate should be able to be used by project members long beyond the deadlines of the project.

*Notes Tool* Having spent a day at Harvard's Radcliffe College several years ago at the "Take Note" conference on the history and future of the note (Nov. 2, 2012), I am well aware that notes are no trivial matter. I would define a note as something that needs to be remembered. A note can relate to any part of a project. In terms of where to store a note, my vote is to put it close to the things it relates to and/or in the place where others will need to go to find its information. Notes may be stored in QDAS or Reference Managers, as well as communication or data storage tools, depending on what makes the most sense.

Personally, I have also found the need for an actual Note tool. I use this tool for interesting and relevant things I am accumulating from the internet related to my topic that I am not sure what to do with yet. In other words, I am not yet ready to say they should be formally entered into the project system. I also use the Note tool for simply taking notes—making lists, jotting items—that are still more for me than anyone else working on the project.

There are diverse options available, two of the best-known today are Evernote and OneNote, but there are many others. In addition, many of these tools are developing collaborative capacities that project teams will find of value. The websites and blogs of the individual tools offer important information on how their capabilities can be applied.

### Qualitative Research Data and Organization Management

Digital tools for the organization and use of qualitative research data come in the form of packages called Qualitative Data Analysis Software (QDAS).

*Qualitative Data Analysis Software (QDAS)* QDAS are necessary anchors for building a robust qualitative research database. Designed and built by qualitative researchers for qualitative researchers, they possess the necessary components for what the researcher will need to do. When trying to conduct research with multiple team members, as well as to build a database to serve the needs of the future, you have to use the right tools (Davidson, Paulus, & Jackson, 2016).

Some qualitative researchers have made objections to these tools, complaining that the technology affordances (or lack thereof) will dictate research choices. It is important to keep in mind that it is the researchers who are in charge of the key decisions about philosophy, approach, research design, etc., not the software, and particularly with team-based research, it is the researchers who must come to grips with their potentially divergent viewpoints, not the software (Garland et al., 2006; di Gregorio & Davidson, 2008). Which QDAS package a team selects doesn't matter, as long as it is robust enough for the tasks for which it will be used.

It is also critical that those who will use the software, as well as those who lead them, learn to read and write fluently using best practices for using the e-project. (Davidson & di Gregorio, 2011). Although the learning curve can be steep, the benefits outweigh the complaints. Once fluent in QDAS, one gains great flexibility and capacity as a researcher. This is what will make investing in the time, professional development, consulting, and cost of the software pay off down the line.

*Managing Internal Organization of the QDAS Database* With large amounts of textual material, it is essential to develop some kind of internal organization. I am using the term "textual" in this discussion in the broadest sense of the word, to include written, audio, visual, and any other material with narrative content that is being archived and organized for use by one or many. In other words, you should not throw all of your data into one big box to be examined later. Rather, as you collect items, they should be placed in different containers and labeled in a meaningful way.

Whole pieces of data should be given one global label, and then these larger pieces of data should then be categorized internally into smaller pieces. The goal of categorization or labeling is to be able to organize materials so they can be found and used again.

This identification and labeling process is most often referred to as "coding" by qualitative researchers, but it has many similarities to such notions as indexing (bibliographies and books) or tagging (web-based practices). In this text, I will be using the terms *coding, indexing,* and *labeling* interchangeably. I will use the term *nodes* to refer specifically to codes as they occur in NVivo software.

In qualitative research with teams, it is important that the labeling process be systematic, and the form it takes must be robust, meaning the codes applied can be clearly defined and are well understood by all team members. This is important for several reasons. With many team members engaged in the labeling process, clarity of the process and the meaning of the codes is important if materials are going to be stored in places where they can be found again by multiple members. Moreover, discussion regarding definition of these labels is a highly creative act that will move interpretation forward in important ways.

This does not mean the coding system has to necessarily be rigid and solely deductive (meaning top-down and established *a priori*). The flexibility of coding will vary with the perspective of the research team. It is also true that even within these parameters, researchers continue to dicker with the right words and the meaning they ascribe to particular codes (Anders & Lester, 2015). Indeed, new visualization tools allow for different forms of "seeing" that can be disruptive and challenging, leading to the development of new meaning, and, thus, new codes (Jackson, 2014a, 2014b).

Even with a small amount of qualitative research data—of one or many forms—the organizational overload builds very quickly. For this reason, especially when working with several researchers, it is critical that there be good timelines and staff with adequate time devoted to processing materials. The processing of research materials should include regular opportunities for review of coding decisions (Sanders & Cuneo, 2010).

Review of coding work is facilitated in QDAS in a variety of ways. Most QDAS software distinguishes among coders, allowing a reviewer to see who is coding what, and in what manner they are coding. Coding properties (a location defined by the software) is a place to record the definitions applied to codes. The QDAS package should also provide a log in which technical changes can be reviewed.

In addition to whatever log the software stores automatically, I strongly recommend that each researcher keep an ongoing methodological log in which methodological decisions are recorded and discussed. In later write-ups, this methodological log will prove invaluable in describing new procedures and discussing how they came into being. Examples of these two forms of logs can be seen in the Appendices C and D.

As the project moves forward and certain categories gain in importance, team leaders will probably assign members to review specific codes and document their findings in memos that can be attached to the code itself, where it can be easily found and reviewed by other team members.

## QDAS and Reference Managers

QDAS and Reference Managers have important features in common. For this reason, some researchers might conclude that they should just select one to use, but that would not be a good idea. It is true that Reference Managers like QDAS tools can handle a range of reference materials, and like QDAS tools, Reference Managers also possess various annotation features. Both tools possess significant capacity in regard to internal searches. Another useful feature that is available in both is the ability to segment a project into smaller projects for export or import, allowing one to use components and structures from one project in the building of another.

However, there are also significant differences that need to be understood before one dives into making decisions about selecting one versus another. QDAS tools are unique in that they allow materials to be coded within the document, not just across documents. At the current moment, Reference Managers can group and categorize or search for keywords, but they cannot code within a document as QDAS does. Reference tools, however, trump QDAS in their ability to cite references in a word processing document, as well as in their ability to search and store library bibliographies.

The most efficient long-term solution I have found is to use both together—QDAS and/with a Reference Manager. My Reference Manager serves as the big bin for large-scale sorting and is the key tool to link references to final text, and QDAS is where I work with a smaller amount of materials for my close reading.

### QDAS and Collaborative Features

Probably the biggest challenge to QDAS users at this moment is related to its collaborative features. Most QDAS available today were developed in the era of stand-alone software, and their collaborative features are slim to primitive. One can copy and send the digital project to a colleague, or, in some brands, one can merge projects (often a painful and confusing process). NVivo allows for the purchase of a dedicated server with virtual-keys for project team members, a feature that may not allow access to the project by those outside a specific institution.

Tools like Dedoose, a newcomer on the scene, offer newer cloud-based options, but in the process raise new questions about ownership, security, and pricing. QDAS software developers are very aware of users' desires for improved collaboration features in their tools, and I would not be going out on a limb to say that the forms and possibilities of research in cloud-based environments will be changing soon.

Because of the rapidly evolving state of collaborative capacities in QDAS, it is critical that team leaders make a systematic evaluation of their collaborative needs in light of current QDAS capabilities. Whichever tool you select will have capabilities and challenges, and you need to know you have workarounds for the obstacles you encounter. Moreover, your workarounds should not overly strain the team, lead to lost materials, or otherwise impede progress. As can be said for every digital drawback—new solutions are on the way!

## Integrating Research Design with Data Archiving Plan

Archiving data has long been significant for quantitative researchers, but it is now also becoming so for qualitative researchers. We are moving into an era where not only will our selected results be made available through papers and conference papers, but all of the materials and processes of a project will also be visible for viewing through deposit in public data repositories.

The movement to support archiving qualitative research data increased in velocity when the United States, the European Union, and other national and global organizations began to mandate archiving of this form of data. Once this occurred, there was no going back. As a result, digital databases of various sorts have emerged to create enduring, well managed archives of research materials. In the United States, for instance, there is the Inter-University Consortium for Political and Social Research (ICPSR) at the Institute of Social Research of the University of Michigan, which contains some qualitative data materials (ICPSR, 2017). More recently, there is the Qualitative Data Repository (QDR) that has been developed at the Center for Qualitative and Multi-Method Inquiry at the University of Syracuse ("Center for Qualitative and Multi-Method Inquiry," 2017). The United Kingdom has been a leader in this field, with the development of Qualibank, a component of the UK Data Service (2017). Another example of a qualitative data archive is the Irish Qualitative Data Archive established at Maynooth University ("Irish Qualitative Data Archive," 2017). These are only a few of the emerging locations for responsible, long-term storage of qualitative data.

Because of these changing circumstances, it is essential that researchers, from the initiation of project planning, think of their data systems as both database and archive. They will use the database they build for the project work in which they are currently engaged, but they, or others, may also use it in the future for subsequent projects, relying on secondary data analysis. This will require archiving (Corti, 2011; Cliggett, 2013).

In order to plan appropriately for archiving the work, a research team should include someone with expertise such as a librarian and/or information specialist, either as a team member or as a consultant. Many of the emerging data repositories can play this role for research teams, weighing in on the development of grants for projects that will store their data at the repository. The repository will approve the archiving plan, providing grantees with a guarantee that this work can be accomplished. Grantees benefit from archiving because it allows their project and its results to have a wider and longer reach. With archived projects, not only are research products cited, but the actual project data can be used by others and cited by others.

### *Archiving Data vs. Archiving QDAS: Transitional Challenges*

Data repositories are comfortable archiving written, audio, and visual texts in commonly available formats. However, data repositories are currently at a standstill in regard to the archiving of qualitative research data that is organized within QDAS. This is due to the multiple forms of QDAS and the lack of a software language that will allow programs to be translated back and forth with ease. As it stands today, projects archived within a QDAS shell will only be useable if the researcher or repository has access to the particular version of QDAS in which the materials are stored—an unlikely proposition at best with the rapid evolution of this software. This means that, although technology has the capacity to allow us to review the organization of a project—coding and analysis—this can only occur in limited circumstances.

As qualitative researchers become more fluent in reading QDAS projects, we can assume that they will also become more interested in seeing that data repositories address this issue. Indeed, at the August 2016 KWALitatief ONderzoek (KWALON) conference in

Holland, software developers and QDAS trainers and leaders begin steps toward making this possible (Evers, 2018).

## Caring: Internalized and Externalized

"Caring," as I am referring to it, is the cherishing of self and other, and the making manifest of that cherishing through attention to attitudes and systematic processes that will maintain safety for both. Caring provides an essential anchor around which to organize teamwork, and a necessary lens through which to screen decisions with study participants. As such, caring composes a connected system of trust, relationship . . . and caring!

Caring as I am describing it comes in two forms. There is internalized caring, where we attend to reflection on self and other, both individually and within the group or team. There is also externalized caring, in which we establish the ethical procedures by which we will keep self and other safe. Caring, whether internal or external, is about living in relationship in a trusting way. To behave in a caring way is to manage your emotions in support of yourself and others so the work can be conducted in a productive manner that will not cause harm to yourself or others.

These perspectives establish a grounded place for work with the team and the participants in the study. First, we will care—for ourselves and others—and second, we will recognize ethics as something more than the mere mechanical response to an IRB: as an ongoing extension of our caring. Self-reflection as part of the ethics of caring for oneself and others will be a continuous part of the work of each individual team member and the team as a whole.

## Internalized Caring: Subjectivities and Self/Group Reflection

Where there is the research self, there is the research other, and vice-versa. To each research situation, we bring our multiple subjectivities—who we are, what we believe, what we have experienced—and these are in constant interaction in our own minds with the topic of inquiry (Peshkin, 1997, p. 1991). For that reason, it is critical that we mine these subjectivities for the good and the bad, as resources and as potential challenges.

Writing about our subjectivities is a task for all team members. It may be used as a starting point for team-formation process. Visual or kinesthetic techniques of different sorts are powerful for eliciting information on our subjectivities. These can include the development of personal posters, or sharing of a small curated collection of items or photographs. Techniques such as logo play can also provide tools for exploration, combining the visual and material in productive ways (Coffey, 2016; Griffin, 2011; Kuhn & Davidson, 2007).

A researcher working alone or with a group would be well counselled to conduct ongoing emotional journaling. Emotional journaling is necessary not only to ensure one is adequately reflective of ethical issues affecting others, but also that one is attending to one's own feelings, sadness, losses, and other emotions that may accompany qualitative research work. Malacrida (2007, p. 1330) argues for the use of reflective tools to support "an ethics of emotional care and support for research team members."

The consideration of self-care—or in the case of complex qualitative research teams, team care—is one that has often been overlooked by researchers, who are often self-sacrificing members of the nonprofit world, but its importance should not be overlooked ("Beth's Blog," 2017).

## Externalized Caring: Ethics and Documentation

Ethics are a formal response to issues of relationship and are construed as semiformal (social norms) or highly formal (legal). Writing helps to define and make sense of these relationships, whether semiformal or formal in nature. Research projects are filled with multiple relationships of which methodological writing will help you (and the team) to make sense. Writing and submitting the IRB proposal is only the tip of the iceberg as far as ethics and ethical writing is concerned. Ethics are everyone's business. No one is exempt from the demands of ethics. Another way to express this would be to say that writing about ethics is part of the doing of ethics.

The writing about ethics includes a range of formal forms of writing that are well grounded in the forms of informal writing described herein. Formal forms of writing about ethics include the research proposal with description of methods and description of access and the informed consent process. It may also include dissertations, journal articles, or books, in which the researcher(s) discuss these issues as well as considerations related to subjectivity, reciprocity, or publication agreements within the group as well as with participants.

The development of a project's formal ethical documents is closely related to all other aspects of the project, from formation of the question, to selection of site and tools for inquiry, and conduct of analysis. The ethical ideals that will guide the project are like a lens through which team members should view all project work. The formal documents created to express these ideals, which are submitted to an IRB or its equivalent (whether within or outside of an organization, such as with use of an outsourced IRB group) are the place where these ideals are made concrete through descriptions of procedures and structures that will address ethical concerns.

For some decades now, government-sponsored research has required IRB approval. Because government-funded research makes some of the largest research awards, this practice has put ethical compliance front and center among researchers. Another concrete sign of the importance of ethical compliance can also be seen in the emerging practice found in an increasing number of peer-reviewed journals, where authors are required to provide a statement that confirms the research described in the article was submitted to, and approved by, a legitimate IRB, and meets required standards for research conducted with human subjects.

In developing the ethical documents for a project, unless the research project is simply replicating materials from an earlier, similar project, there is usually a significant amount of back and forth discussion between researchers and IRB staff as the details of the new project get hammered out. Even with a project making use of prior forms, there have often been changes in IRB procedures, requiring changes and more detail in new rounds of scrutiny. The IRB staff will serve as a conduit for comments made by IRB panel members, helping applicants to address concerns.

Development of the ethical documents required for a project requires a good, close working relationship with the individuals working in the IRB.

For these reasons, it is extremely important that we treat IRB staff with respect and with recognition for the professional work they are doing to help the research team meet these goals. Resentment towards IRB staff and requirements may be justified in a few cases, but more often it springs from a researcher's impatience, and, unfortunately, may be related to a researcher's desire for quick recognition, versus their real job—which is to care and serve. Undue impatience with ethics procedures should be questioned and in some extreme cases may be viewed as an illustration of what will be overall problematic behavior for the research team, requiring early intervention.

Team-based qualitative researchers will make their lives easier by ensuring everything required for ethical conduct of a project is well organized, and where possible, standardized statements are ready and waiting to be dropped into the necessary documents. In the early stages of the project, it is important to designate an area in shared electronic storage and/or QDAS project in which to place all ethics-related documents. These might include:

- Human subject certifications
- Informed consent forms
- IRB proposals and any addenda
- Revisions to any documents

These items should be easy for the appropriate research team members to get to in case they need to be accessed or referenced.

## Conclusion: Initiating Projects Through Writing

Many forms of writing have been described here that are critical to the work of initiating a complex team research project using qualitative research methods. There are the innumerable emails as one is sorting out teams and team members, initiating ideas, and setting tasks, the minutes of meetings or drafts of proposals through the development of a final proposal, project description, or research brief (which will describe writing about both the substance of the issue and the methodology). There are also the forms and protocols for the IRB, the internal and external agreements and descriptions of procedures, as well as such items as job descriptions, if new members are to be hired. As the team establishes itself, there is also writing about one's subjectivities and relationship to the project work or the site. Another writing task is the drafting of the database shell, importation of key items, variables, preliminary coding decisions, and initiation of the methodology log.

Quantified, this is a significant amount of writing that is often discounted by researchers who may think writing up the results or findings is the real writing of a project. This initial writing, however, is highly significant to the outcome of the entire project. It contains the conceptualization, rationale, and plan for what will come.

It is important not only to hold onto this writing as documentation of the project, but also to document the process by which the writing up of the research design phase unfolded. An ongoing log or memo will be useful, as well as memos in which key decisions or ideas are documented for future review. While this will be important to all forms of research, in qualitative research, this documentation is particularly important to support methodological analysis. The electronic database can serve as an invaluable aid in regard to organizing and storing these materials and providing easy access to them at later points.

## References

Anders, Allison Daniel, and Jessica Nina Lester. 2015. "Lessons from Interdisciplinary Qualitative Research: Learning to Work Against a Single Story." *Qualitative Research* 15 (6): 738.
"Beth's Blog." 2017. http://www.bethkanter.org.
Buhlman, Beat. 2006. *Need to Manage a Virtual Team? Theory and Practice in a Nutshell.* Zug, Switzerland: Cuvillier Verlag.
"Center for Qualitative and Multi-Method Inquiry." 2017. https://www.maxwell.syr.edu/cqmi.aspx.
Cliggett, Lisa. 2013. "Qualitative Data Archiving in the Digital Age: Strategies for Data Preservation and Sharing." *The Qualitative Report* 18 (How to Art. 1): 1–11.
Coffey, Amanda. 2016. "Review of The Ethnographic Self as Resource: Writing Memory and Experience into Ethnography." *Qualitative Research* 16 (3): 353–354. doi:10.1177/1468794115571701
Corti, Louise. 2011. "The European Landscape of Qualitative Social Research Archives: Methodological and Practical Issues." *Forum: Qualitative Social Research* 12 (3): Art. 11.

Creamer, Elizabeth. 2003. "Interpretive Processes in Collaborative Research." *Academic Exchange Quarterly* 7 (3): 179–183. ISSN 1096-1453.

Curry, Leslie A., Alicia O'Cathain, Vicki L. Plano Clark, Rosalie Aroni, Michael Fetters, and David Berg. 2012. "The Role of Group Dynamics in Mixed Methods Health Sciences Research Teams." *Journal of Mixed Methods Research* 6 (1): 5.

Davidson, Judith, and Silvana di Gregorio. 2011. "Qualitative Research and Technology: In the Midst of a Revolution." In *The Sage Handbook of Qualitative Research*, edited by Norman K. Denzin and Yvonna S. Lincoln, 627–643. Los Angeles, CA: Sage Publications.

Davidson, Judith, Trena Paulus, and Kristi Jackson. 2016. "Speculating on the Future of Digital Tools for Qualitative Research." *Qualitative Inquiry* (7): 606.

di Gregorio, Silvana, and Judith Davidson. 2008. *Qualitative Research Design for Software Users*. Maidenhead, Berkshire: Open University Press, 2008.

Eubanks, Dawn L., Michael Palanski, Joy Olabisi, Adam Joinson, and James Dove. 2016. "Team Dynamics in Virtual, Partially Distributed Teams: Optimal Role Fulfillment." *Computers in Human Behavior* 61: 556–568. doi:10.1016/j.chb.2016.03.035

Evers, Jeanine C. 2018. "Current issues in qualitative data analysis software (QDAS): A user and developer perspective." *The Qualitative Report* 23 (13): Art 5.

Garland, Diana R., Mary Katherine O'Connor, Terry A. Wolfer, and F. Ellen Netting. 2006. "Team-based Research." *Qualitative Social Work* 5 (1): 93.

Griffin, Meredith. 2011. "Review of Writing Qualitative Inquiry: Self, Stories, and Academic Life." *Qualitative Research* 11 (2): 219–220. doi:10.1177/14687941110110020604

Harris, Andrew J., Judith Davidson, Elizabeth Letourneau, Carl Paternite, and Karin Tusinski Miofsky. 2013. Building a Prevention Framework to Address Teen "Sexting" Behaviors. Washington, D.C.: U.S. Department of Justice.

Hesse-Biber, Sharlene, Deborah Rodriguez, and Nollaig A. Frost. 2015. "A Qualitatively Driven Approach to Multimethod and Mixed Methods Research." In *The Oxford Handbook of Multimethod and Mixed Methods Research Inquiry*, edited by Sharlene Hesse-Biber and R. Burke Johnson, 3–20. Oxford, UK: Oxford University Press.

"ICPSR." 2017. http://www.icpsr.umich.edu/icpsrweb/.

"Irish Qualitative Data Archive." 2017. Maynooth University, accessed August 14. https://www.maynoothuniversity.ie/iqda.

Jackson, Kristi. 2014a. "Qualitative Data Analysis Software, Visualizations, and Transparency: Toward an Understanding of Transparency in Motion." Computer Assisted Qualitative Data Analysis Surrey, England, May 3, 2014.

Jackson, Kristi. 2014b. "Qualitative Methods, Transparency, and Qualitative Data Analysis Software: Toward an Understanding of Transparency in Motion." Unpublished Dissertation, 2014.

Kuhn, Sarah, and Judith Davidson. 2007. "Thinking with Things, Teaching with Things: Enhancing Student Learning in Qualitative Research Through Reflective Use of Tools and Materials." *Qualitative Research Journal* 7 (2): 63–75.

Lubke, Jennifer, Virginia G. Britt, Trena Paulus, and David Atkins. 2017. "Hacking the Literature Review: Opportunities and Innovations to Improve the Research Process." *Reference and User Services Quarterly* 56 (4): 285–295.

Lungeanu, A., Y. Huang, and N. S. Contractor. 2014. "Understanding the Assembly of Interdisciplinary Teams and Its Impact on Performance." *Journal of Informetrics* 8 (1): 59–70. doi:10.1016/j.joi.2013.10.006

Malacrida, Claudia. 2007. "Reflexive Journaling on Emotional Research Topics: Ethical Issues for Team Researchers." *Qualitative Health Research* 17 (10): 1329.

Mauthner, Natasha S., and Andrea Doucet. 2008. "'Knowledge Once Divided Can Be Hard to Put Together Again': An Epistemological Critique of Collaborative and Team-Based Research Practices." *Sociology* 42 (5): 971.

Paulus, Trena, Jessica Nina Lester, and Paul G. Dempster. 2014. *Digital Tools for Qualitative Research*. Thousand Oaks, CA: Sage.

Peshkin, Alan. 1991. *The Color of Strangers, The Color of Friends: The Play of Ethnicity in School and Community*. Chicago, IL: University of Chicago Press.

Peshkin, Alan. 1997. *Places of Memory: Whiteman's Schools and Native American Communities*. Mahwah, NJ: Lawrence Erlbaum Associates, Publishers.

Sanders, Carrie B., and Carl J. Cuneo. 2010. "Social Reliability in Qualitative Team Research." *Sociology* 44 (2): 325–343. doi:10.1177/0038038509357194

"UK Data Service Discover » UK QualiBank." 2017. https://discover.ukdataservice. ac.uk/QualiBank.

Wasser, Judith Davidson, and Liora Bresler. 1996. "Working in the Interpretive Zone: Conceptualizing Collaboration in Qualitative Research Teams." *Educational Researcher* 25 (5): 5–15.

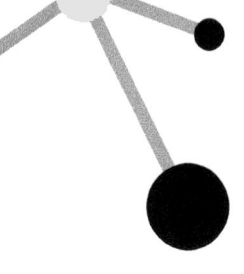

# WRITING UP METHODS IN TEAM-BASED QUALITATIVE RESEARCH

THE FOCUS of this chapter is on the critical task of writing up methodology. The chapter illustrates the ways researchers must attend to methodological issues—from the initiation of the project through its completion—in order to be able to do the writing up. It provides information on techniques for keeping the methodological account current and informative so that it can provide support for demonstrating the overall quality of the project and its trustworthiness. This approach also helps the team to capture and reflect upon the unique methodological knowledge it has gleaned through its work—one of the treasures of every qualitative research project undertaken.

As a form of research that relies deeply on writing processes, it stands to reason that qualitative research has a special commitment to writing up its method. All researchers must attend to method, but lacking numerical formulas, qualitative research is particularly committed to paying careful, documented attention to the methodological process and its relationship to the question, the site, and fellow researchers. For these reasons, our methodological documentation must be thorough, detailed, reflective, and ongoing. Teams, however, by their size and variability, complicate the collection of such methodological data and the telling of the methodological story. Methodological descriptions have a long history in qualitative research as providing the proxies for trustworthiness of results by offering a transparency that often stands as a signifier for quality. Two key points methodological documentation can provide insight for are: (1) considerations of subjectivity, ethics, and research relationships; and (2) trustworthiness, meaning an assessment of scope, turning points, and judgment (Altheide & Johnson, 1994). Methodological documentation, thus, informs substantive findings and visa-versa. Moreover, methodological documentation must be integrated with substantive documentation if the team is to make any sense of the project.

There are many techniques for methodological documentation that lead to good methodological writing. By attending to these issues as the project is initiated, you will not be caught short later when subsequent writing tasks require methodological information. This chapter will provide ample detail on those techniques and how they can be integrated into the inquiry and the team's work.

For the hardcore qualitative researcher, methodological writing can also be an area of deep aesthetic interest and enjoyment. Through methodology, one expresses one's style and approach as a researcher. It is internally rewarding, and good methodological writing brings joy to other writers with similar interests.

## Methods: In-Process, Ideal, and Methodological Literature

There are three critical forms of methodological writing qualitative researchers must attend to—the methodological writing that occurs throughout the course of the project (*in process*), the standardized description of the methodological process (*ideal*), and scholarly writing that probes a methodological conundrum (*methodological literature*). The three are defined next.

*Methods in process* include the database or curated collection of research materials, which will include coding, memos, multiple forms of data, notes from interpretive meetings, informal papers, and other items. These should be kept in the database where they can be accessed to support methodological or substantive work. Even in relatively small qualitative research projects, these combined pieces of writing add up to significant amounts. In team-based research, different members of the team will have different roles in regard to production of the in-process methodological documentation.

*Methods in the ideal form* include the description of the methodology as it is dropped into multiple products that are disseminated by the project. These are developed as needed. At the beginning of a project, member(s) of a team may develop a standard or generic description of the method as it is imagined before the project has unfolded. These descriptions are frequently redeveloped as the project moves forward and more elements of the completed method are available to describe. On a complex team, the standardized account is usually written by the principal investigators (PIs) or a senior member in charge of methodology. In a less hierarchical project scheme, the responsibility may shift among members, depending upon the audience for the description.

*Methodological literature* refers to presentations, papers, or other products that the team produces as a reflection upon their methodological approaches. During or after a project is concluded, in addition to substantive findings, teams may also identify methodological findings. Methodological findings may be important turning points in the research work deserving of thoughtful reflection, and it may be useful to share these with a wider professional audience, which is the purpose of methodological literature. Not only is methodology the topic of books from a variety of publishers, but there is a growing number of journals specializing in issues related to qualitative research methodology.

Any team member may express the desire or interest to write in depth about a qualitative research quandary emerging in the course of the study, although the idea will probably be initiated by team members with the greatest depth of interest in qualitative research. The writing up may be confined to a few members or may include the full team. Depending on the issue and approach, junior members as well as experienced researchers may all have insights to contribute.

In the following sections, the preparation and development of each of these three forms of methodological writing is described in greater depth.

## Methods in Process

Your research design should set you up to be ready to be successful as a documenter of methods in process. Important tools you will be using for this work include:

1. **Your capacity for reflexivity**—meaning the capacity to reflect on self and other and back to self again in seeking to identify and understand methodological development. The expression of reflexivity can be seen in many components of the writing—from bracketed asides in interviews or observations, or the quality of methodological logs or memos.
2. Various **bins for methodological ideas**. These would include:
   a. A methodological log
   b. Coding related to methodological concerns
   c. Memos on methodological issues
   d. Ongoing development of a methodological library
   e. Periodic methodological reviews that consolidate your understanding of methodological progress up to that point

### Capacity for Reflexivity

A qualitative researcher's capacity for reflexivity is important to every aspect of their work—from research design to ethics, and from data collection to analysis and representation. Everything depends upon this ability to attend to the behaviors and practices of other and self in a cyclical, ongoing manner. Reflexivity also depends upon writing, as a key analytical tool. We note or identify an issue by writing about it, then inquire further through more writing. Eventually, we come to interpret or understand the concern through the writing we have done about it.

Notions of reflexivity have travelled far over the last few decades of qualitative research history. Feminist and post-positivist writers have helped to illustrate the importance of reflexivity in all pieces of the research process. This is a shift from an earlier, limited notion of reflexivity as a tool that would be occasionally useful (Siltanen, Willis, & Scobie, 2008).

Just as earlier descriptions about qualitative research focused on single researchers, so, too, discussions of reflexivity were treated as individual matters, and there was little information available on reflexive processes of team-based research (Siltanen, Willis, & Scobie, 2008). Siltanen, Willis, and Scobie (2008, p. 47) refer to "the interpretive opportunities created by reflexively addressing the other within the research team, and the possibility of forging a common understanding of the research subject research subject/object."

We store this writing in a number of "bins," which are usually found in the symbolic "pantry" or "larder" of the practicing qualitative researcher.

### Bins for Methodological Ideas

Methodological Log

Methodological logs, as described earlier, are a place for the researcher's ongoing documentation of methodological decisions and the reasoning or circumstances surrounding these decisions. I have been making use of methodological logs since I was in graduate school (thanks to the example of Alan [Buddy] Peshkin, a highly influential teacher in my life; Eisner, 2007). In working on my dissertation, I filled four notebooks with jottings on methodological issues that I analyzed by paginating, coding, and creating coding summaries on large notecards (Davidson, 2000). I was formally introduced to QDAS in 1997 in the form of Non-numerical Unstructured Data Indexing Searching and Theorizing (NUD*IST) and quickly translated my hard-copy practice of methodological logging into a digital form, using the memo function. Since 1998, as a teacher of qualitative research, I have regularly assigned methodological logs in some form to my students. Over my years of experience working on different forms of team-based research, I have always kept methodological logs for the projects on which I have worked. These records contain important documentation from which I build other methodological components.

On a complex project, the keeping of the methodological log can take a variety of forms. On a project in which all team members are charged with the conduct of qualitative research, all should be expected to keep a methodological log. In a complex project in which only a few members or one member is in charge of conducting the qualitative research component, at the very least, I would expect the qualitative research members to keep methodological logs for their work.

A methodological log can be a spiral-bound notebook, a word-processing file, or a specially designated memo in the QDAS project. Whichever form you use, keep it open and available whenever you are working on your project.

If, as I recommend, the qualitative research team is working in a QDAS program, the program itself will keep an ongoing technical log, which is helpful to access when you are picking up after a time away from the project or want to check actions that have been taken. This technical log, however, cannot substitute for the researcher's own methodological log. (See the Appendices C and D for examples of methodological log and project event log in QDAS.)

Your methodological log is the place to store your methodological progress: What have you done on the project? What did you accomplish today? It is also a place to reflect on your methodological process: How did you conduct your activities? How did the work unfold? Finally, it is a place to evaluate and reflect: What did you learn? What could you suggest to others? Are you going to modify or adapt at this point?

As you are keeping track of these three items: (1) action, (2) process, and (3) evaluation/reflection, you are, by virtue of the task, attending to methodological turning points. In other words, what methodological decisions are you making? When do these arise? What is the context in which the turning point occurs? How is your reaction shaped by your training and beliefs? How does this incident reflect the views of the participants in the study or your co-researchers?

Two key intertwined methodological points that are at the heart of decision-making are the topics of subjectivity and ethics (see "Caring: Internal and External" in Chapter 2). By subjectivity, I am referring here to your beliefs, assumptions, and identities. At what points do your subjectiviti(es) become ignited or disconnected?

Why? What do you like or dislike when you are at the site or talking to participants? Those are important places to probe yourself—here you have the opportunity to use yourself as a resource, as well as to explore issues that could cause you problems at the site or among team members if ignored (Peshkin, 1997, 1991).

Issues of subjectivity are closely connected to ethics—interrogating your interactions with the site and its members is a critical part of the ongoing work of maintaining an ethical position that will protect you and the site participants. For instance, have issues arisen that complicate the promises you made in your informed consent process? How should these be solved? Or, did you witness something that is legally unacceptable at the site? Do you have a mandate to report this issue? The methodological log is a safe place for you to identify and sort out these concerns. The better the record you keep of emerging ethical concerns, the more appropriately you can respond to them.

When working on a team, make a regular habit of combing the methodological log for questions that can be added as agenda items for the next team meeting. Discussion of methodological issues is methodology in the making. Few things can be found to be right or wrong. Each item raised will be the beginning point of new methodological thinking that the group will gradually decipher, define, and act upon. These discussions are critical starting points for the writing of the methodological progress of the study.

### Coding Methodological Issues

Coding for methodological issues simply means paying attention to where in your data and your experiences with the project you find yourself questioning, intrigued, and generally paying specific attention to methodology. Methodological coding may start simply with a single code for methodology. If you are reading interview transcripts in hard copy, you may note "methodology" in the margins, when you note something related to the topic. If you are working in a QDAS project, you can make a code for the general term "methodology" that you apply to the parts of a text that raise relevant methodological questions.

Upon reviewing the places where you have coded for the broad category of methodology, you may find the contents of that one code are diverse. Some of the mentions may relate to data collection, others to your subjectivities, and still other items are related to concerns about validity. You are free to subdivide the category of methodology to create more specific methodological codes. You may also want to periodically review the methodological log and code items you find there that are deserving of greater methodological attention.

Team-based projects, whether fully or partially devoted to working with qualitative research data, will benefit greatly through continuous methodological monitoring of this sort. Keeping a methodological log, scanning materials and experiences to identify emergent methodological issues, and bringing these to the attention of fellow team members are critical parts of growing the methodological component of a team-based qualitative research project. Every time a methodological issue is brought to the group, it becomes an opportunity for learning. Senior members can learn from junior researchers, and vice-versa; quantitative researchers can learn from qualitative researchers, and vice-versa; and members of different disciplines can chime in with the ways their discipline has approached the concern.

Methodological Memos

You won't get too far into your methodological logging and coding before you find that the documenting of some specific methodological issue is growing exponentially. This issue compels you to think and write about it at length. It may be an issue related to data collection, or a tricky ethical issue. Perhaps your initial exploration of it leads you to thinking about some key literature in that area, and some further comparisons. You realize your log is in danger of becoming overwhelmed by writing about this one issue. This is the point at which you stop—and create a memo on this topic (Emerson, Fretz, & Shaw, 1995).

If you are working in a word-processing program, simply open up a new file, title it appropriately, cut and paste the material on this topic from the methodological log, and get to work writing more on this topic. If you are working in QDAS, most software programs will provide you with an area of files that are classified as memos with options to link these files to places in texts or entire documents for easy access from multiple locations.

Methodological memos are places where you begin to explore a methodological issue in depth. You will probably know ahead of time some of the issues you will want to investigate through writing a memo. For instance, at the start of a project, some researchers will automatically create a memo about each form of data they collect (interviews, observations, artifacts), knowing they will need to discuss the methodological issues each form raises. For me, the topic of subjectivities and ethics is something I know I will want to track from the beginning, and I will have a blank memo ready on this topic.

Many of the methodological memos you create, however, will not have a one-to-one correspondence with a pre-established task or concept in research. Instead, they will grow up in the cracks among concepts or tasks. This is where the excitement of methodological writing begins to emerge as you find you are treading on new ground, exploring new territory.

For team-based research, methodological memoing can take many forms. Individuals may be encouraged to keep such memos linked to the methodological codes they are developing (a process easily done in QDAS). Team discussions (on email, in group phone calls, or in face-to-face meetings) will also include discussion of methodological issues that can be strained out to become a joint methodological memo—fixing the findings of that moment or a specific discussion in a document.

Methodological logs, codes, and memos have in them the seeds of future methodological writing—either the ideal examples of the methodology that become part of various papers and reports, or the more extensive form of methodological literature. These forms of in-process methodological writing are critical to develop in tandem with what team members view as the substantive work of the project. Failure to keep methodological and substantive reflection linked and on pace will be problematic as the project proceeds. Without current documentation of methodology, the researcher(s) will lack critical materials necessary to describe the methodological issues related to substantive findings.

### Ongoing Development of a Methodological Library

Collection of methodological literature may not seem like a form of *in process* writing, but it is critical to the development of methodological writing of any sort. By "tuning in" to literature—meaning our more distant methodological friends (outside of the immediate research team and often people that we do not know, may not be alive, but have something vital to say to us about methodological issues), we keep the methodological process vibrant and meaningful (see also Chapter 1 for a description of the category of extant data; Chapter 2 for discussion of Reference Managers and Note tools).

The development of a methodological library, the analysis of its contents, and the integration of those contents with the other materials of the research project are all opportunities for methodological writing. This writing will range from coding of the materials, to writing about the methodological issues raised in key articles or books, and writing about the ways the ideas from methodological experts have relevance to the work of this particular project.

In QDAS, any digital material, whether it be field notes or methodological articles, can be coded using the same coding tools, and, indeed, the same codes. This means methodological literature can operate on the same playing field as project field notes, allowing for dynamic integration among these pieces. The same holds true for the many memos that emerge in the course of a project—they, too, can be broken down (coding and analysis) and juxtaposed or reconnected to other pieces of project materials (recoded, relationships visualized) through QDAS affordances. These technologies allow for a potentially richer integration of materials than is possible from simply trying to hold it all in one brain.

When a researcher downloads formal references in the literature to a QDAS package, depending on the features of the package, a memo containing bibliographic data may also be automatically generated. This memo can be a useful place to begin to make notes about how you want to use the piece of literature with which you are working.

A QDAS project on one topic can be copied so the literature base can be repurposed for another project on a similar topic. As you use the databases from earlier projects to create new QDAS projects, you will see that literature databases from earlier projects are like nest eggs gaining interest. Who knows, in a future world we may make our QDAS databases stocked with methodological literature and its analysis available for use—free or for sale—to other researchers, from which they may build new projects of their own.

Most teams will probably integrate the review of literature about the topic of the project and the methodological literature searches. Thanks to folders and libraries, all materials—methodological or substantive, theoretical or empirical—can be combined or separated with ease within a Reference Manager or QDAS tool.

On some projects, all members will be responsible for some literature-review tasks. On others, they may divide tasks for literature review, depending upon interests and skills. Consider attaching a librarian or information specialist to the team, who can assist with the search and organization of literature for the project.

As with all things related to the database of the project (whether in a QDAS project or not), careful attention should be given to the filing and tagging system, so that the materials can be retrieved easily. These systems need to be flexibly designed so that materials can be accessed from several different angles.

### Periodic Methodological Review

Periodic methodological reviews offer another opportunity to investigate methodological topics. Doing this at specific times over the course of the project will allow you (and your team) to surface important concerns and to adjust and create solutions that will allow the project to move forward more smoothly. Methodological reviews ensure that methodological in-process writing is keeping pace with developments on the substantive side, and vice-versa.

### Self and Team Review

A self-conducted review of the methodological progress of a project (or one's individual work on a project) may be as simple as a review of the methodological log you have kept of the project. Although the contents are already familiar, in reviewing them, you may find some issues have moved to the background, and others have moved to the foreground. Such trends may, or may not, be of interest or importance to you and the team.

This is also an opportunity to review the methodology memos and to refine methodological codes. As you review them, you may want to add to them or annotate them with new ideas. You may find that codes need to be renamed and descriptions revised to reflect new understanding.

Making tables, charts, or other visualizations is always an excellent way to consolidate information and help you to prepare for informal or formal presentations on the methodology. If you used visualizations in your initial proposal to describe the methodology, annotating them now is a way to capture what was supposed to happen and what did happen.

A team methodological review is an opportunity to review key milestones you have passed and ask group members to comment upon or annotate important ideas that are related to these methodological milestones. This is a moment where you can ask: What did we do right? What was problematic? What do we need to fix? How can we do that? Make sure to document the discussion and include this documentation as a memo or field note in the larger project.

As with an individual review, any kind of visualization that can be used for the discussion will be helpful. Perhaps the group can create a timeline or brainstorm a list of methodological challenges. Snap a photo of your wall work with your cell phone, and these visualizations can then be added to the project database.

*Semi-Outsider Reviews: Consultants, Advisory Boards, and Funding Agency Discussions* There are also other forms of methodological review that fall in between insider reviews and the development of methodological literature. In your original proposal, your team may have had the foresight to build in the services of a methodological consultant who can work with you across the course of the timeline; or, at a crossroads in your work, the team may seek out a methodological consultant for assistance.

You may have periodic meetings with an expert advisory board at which methodology, as well as substance, will be discussed and suggestions made. On funded projects, program officers from the funding agency may discuss methodological issues with team leaders or the full team, asking thoughtful questions, sharing resources, and offering suggestions. These are all places where methodological thinking and writing will occur.

## Methods in the Ideal Form

Before a project can be initiated, the methodology has to be sketched out in some detail and carefully described. Then at various times during the conduct of the work, project leaders will need to write descriptions that provide an overview of the methodology up to that moment in a clear, succinct manner. These descriptions must convey information about what methodologies were used, the rationale for selecting the ones used, the timeline and scope of data collection, and methods of analysis and interpretation. The writer must offer the maximum amount of information with the minimum of jargon. This will mean different things to different audiences, and each methodological description will need to anticipate the informational needs of that audience.

### *Bare Bones Description*

Think of a bare bones description as a kind of sourdough bread starter that is allowed to sit in the refrigerator from week to week. You pull some out every week to get a new loaf started, and while each loaf over the year shares material from the starter, it is also different and unique as the condition of the starter changes and the baker chooses to add different items to the new batch of bread. The bare bones methodology description is like the sourdough starter, it helps the new methodological descriptions get started, but each one will rise and bake in its own way.

Particularly if you are working on a team, it is useful to have a bare bones methodological description in a special location where it can be easily grabbed for a variety of purposes by different members of the team. Here are the minimum kinds of items that should be included in this description: in Table 3.1, I draw upon the project on views of teen "sexting" that I was involved in to illustrate what a bare bones methodology description might contain (Harris et al., 2013).

As time goes by, any number of items might be added or amended in the bare bones description. For instance, numbers of participants reported may need to change if more participants are added at a later time. Periodically, it is also a good idea to review the description, make notations, and update it, so you will always be up and ready to run with this description.

Table 3.1
**Bare Bones Methodology Description**

| Question or Item | Indication of Response or Example: |
|---|---|
| What kind of methodology was employed for this study? | This was primarily a qualitative research study with some descriptive statistics. |
| Who conducted the study? | It was conducted by an interdisciplinary team of researchers in criminal justice, social psychology, and education, located at three institutions of higher education in three regions of the United States. |
| Where and from whom was information collected?<br><br>(This information is often intertwined with information on data collected.) | Data were collected from three different audiences representing teens, teen caregivers, and other adults who work with teens. The primary sites of data collection for teens and teen caregivers were a collection of three high schools in each of the three regions where the research teams were located. A variety of venues were used to collect data from the other adult category. Teens were interviewed in gender-specific groups—1 male and 1 female group per high school or community organization.<br><br>Data collection was staggered by audience: youth data were collected in the first round; caregiver data in the second round; and other adult data in the third round.<br><br>[After data were collected, we could then report that we interviewed 123 teens, 92 parents or caregivers, and 117 others who worked with adolescents. We were also able to provide details on the ethnic/racial composition of the participants.] |

Table 3.1
**Continued**

| Question or Item | Indication of Response or Example: |
| --- | --- |
| What forms of data were collected? | Focus groups were the primary source of data, supplemented by surveys. Teens, Caregivers, and Other Adults filled out an anonymous demographic survey before the focus group. Only the teens did a survey following the focus group in which they were anonymously asked questions about their experience with sexting. |
| How was the material organized and analyzed? | All data collected were submitted to the lead team, which took primary responsibility for having audiotapes transcribed, and then organizing the data within the NVivo database. |
| | Data were analyzed simultaneously on two fronts. At the local sites, transcripts for that site were read and annotated by the site's lead researchers. At the same time, all transcripts from all sites were read and reviewed by the team at the lead center. Simultaneously, transcripts and participant data were loaded into NVivo. Data were coded initially by interview question, then material within each question area was examined separately for each group. Interpretive meetings of all team members were held as data collection was completed for each of the three groups. The meetings were carefully documented, and the emerging ideas served as the impetus for subsequent analysis of the material. |

(continued)

Table 3.1
**Continued**

| Question or Item | Indication of Response or Example: |
|---|---|
| Are there any special details related to trustworthiness and team functioning? | Two researchers were present at each focus group, one taking the lead in asking questions from the structured interview protocol, and the other making sure that logistical and technical components were running smoothly. As soon as possible after the experience, both wrote their own memos on the process and emergent findings that were submitted to the lead team for review. |
| Ethical statement | The participant materials for this project—from informed consent to survey and focus group protocols—were carefully reviewed by the IRBs of two of the institutions involved (one university already had an institutional agreement with the lead university in regard to IRB processes). |
| | Informed consent for all participants was acquired before the research was undertaken. In the case of youth under 18, parental consent was also sought and received. |
| | Student participants received a gift card of $25.00 for their participation in the focus group interviews. No incentives were provided for adult participation. |

## *A Couple More Hints*

A team membership "cheat sheet" is also very handy. This is a list of all the team members at all sites with correct spelling of names, correct titles, and all contact information. Keep information on all members who have participated in the project, whether they are currently working on it or not. Note name changes and institutional changes as necessary. Larger team projects often span several years, and even the most stable projects will have some change in personnel. The team member cheat sheet can be stored in the same location as the bare bones methodological description.

Also, because much of team research will be funded research, it is very important to keep a statement with the specific language that has to be used on any document related to the project's funder. For instance, in the Sexting Study, we used this statement:

> This project was supported by Grant No. 2010-MC-CX-0001, awarded by the Office of Juvenile Justice and Delinquency Prevention, Office of Justice Programs, U.S. Department of Justice. Points of view or opinions in this document are those of the authors and do not necessarily represent the official position or policies of the U.S.
> Department of Justice. (Harrison et al., 2013, title page)

This statement can be stored with the bare bones methodological description and the team member cheat sheet. With these items close at hand, team members can quickly respond to requests for information from the media, funders, supervisors, or others.

For those working on funded projects, these suggestions may appear to be self-evident. However, for those on non-funded projects or projects with a variety of participant roles, this may be useful information.

## Methodological Literature

Through the daily methodological work team members conduct—logging, coding, writing memos, and participating in a variety of project discussions—substantive and methodological ideas will be given form and substance. A group will not be long into a project before it realizes it is already building a sizeable cache of interesting methodological material that has value to a wider community than just the team members. This methodological material needs to be shared, as indeed, discussion of these ideas is what propels methodology forward within the field of qualitative research.

Sharing methodological insights with professional audiences, receiving useful feedback, and reworking the ideas through interaction with others beyond the research team are important components of increasing the professionalization of qualitative research work. Presentations and workshops, whether with a wider team membership, semi-outsiders (described previously), or another professional audience, can be beginning points for polishing methodological work.

## Ways to Share Methodological Insights

### Beginning Steps

Presentations (including papers, round tables, poster sessions, or other formats) and workshops (how-to sessions and hands-on reflective sessions) offer opportunities for researchers at all career points to take their methodological insights into the wider world. There are many opportunities for presentations—some are simple, low-risk, and local; others are more complicated, higher risk, and to a broader audience. In today's world, these opportunities do not have to be face-to-face, but may be conducted virtually.

Despite the massive changes in higher education and communications, the peer-reviewed journal article is still the gold standard of accomplishment for those in the academic world. In particular, researchers just entering the field are under significant pressure to publish as much as possible in the highest impact peer-reviewed journals, as a single author or a first author. On a research team, senior staff need to support rising researchers to achieve these accomplishments, lest they find themselves without colleagues in the near future! It also behooves those with senior positions to pass the torch of methodological excitement to the new generation. Often when writing about a meaty topic, it is helpful to write about it from several angles, letting different team members take the lead on different aspects of the write-up.

### Writing on a Team

Writing on a team—about methodological or substantive issues—can be very exciting. You will learn about more resources, be challenged in new ways, and the amount and quality of your writing will move forward fast. I have found it works best, however, with some good structure, a designated group leader(s) (depending upon the tasks), and a reasonable timeline. Tasks can be allocated based on individual strengths, interests, or needs (for instance, a team member who needs a publication, or one with a specific passion). There are many resources on the topic of collaborative writing: a good example is *Team Writing: A Guide to Working in Groups* (Wolfe, 2010).

The writing team and the research team may not be composed of all the same members. The writing team may be a sub-team of the larger team, or new teams of writers can form that span the insider/outsider divide. For instance, at your professional conference, you may serve on a panel in which there are four other researchers bringing examples of the methodological issue your research team identified and investigated. The five of you (from five different projects/organizations) decide to collaborate on a methodological article about this issue that spans your five examples. Now you find yourself reporting back about the new methodological writing to the original research team as you work with the new writing team. The ideas emerging in this new insider/outsider writing team provide new insight to the original research team in regard to their methodology. Everyone is nourished by the discussion.

Early on in developing a full article, it is a good idea to examine appropriate journals and identify which ones would be good choices for submission. Author's guidelines will be available online and should be studied at an early stage in the design of an article to make sure time isn't wasted writing to the wrong perspective or in the wrong format.

Today, there are even special digital tools to help you search and identify appropriate journals. An example is the match function in the online version of Endnote, a reference management tool. My doctoral students and I have had great fun creating article titles and abstracts, submitting to this function, and seeing what match is made for us. It has taught us much about the journals in our specific areas of interest. There are many interdisciplinary journals that specialize in publishing qualitative and mixed-methods methodological pieces. Also, don't overlook journals emerging in specific disciplinary areas that are seeking methodological content material. It goes without saying that if the team has been keeping up with the ongoing task of building the literature database for the project, team members will have quick and easy access to the literature they need when it comes time to write the paper.

With methodological writing, as with substantive writing, ownership needs to be defined from the beginning. Key questions in regard to the writing include: Who owns what? Who has the right to write about what? How will authorship be listed? This is when the group charter and decisions about publication made prior to the work getting underway become extremely important.

### Other Forms of Methodological Presentation: The QDAS Project

If you and your team are organizing and analyzing your research materials in a QDAS project, you have devoted significant attention to the development of the project in this form. In digital form, it is the full corpus of the project—data, indexing, literature, inquiries (in many forms), and emergent writing. A well-organized digital project (or e-project) is a thing of beauty to those who know how to read it, meaning that they are able to navigate its form and make sense of the content as it is organized. Increasingly, researchers who make use of QDAS find that presentation of the project itself can be useful for the inside group (the research team) and to outsiders. The e-project is, in and of itself, a methodological product upon which to review and reflect.

In projects where team members have strong QDAS skills, looking at the e-project (projecting it and reviewing together) will be an ongoing part of the work as members make decisions about how it should be organized, where things will be located, how tasks will be divided, and how to work most efficiently. It is also a very important interpretive tool, allowing members to find items quickly, put forward and test hypotheses, and visualize ideas.

In geographically dispersed and semi-virtual teams, linked by professional interest but located at a variety of locations and/or organizations, not all members may have access to QDAS or to the same QDAS package. There are numerous ways the research team members working with the QDAS package can deal with these circumstances. Parts of the project can be exported to significant others who need to review emerging findings in the form of data chunks, whether or not they have access to the QDAS package itself. In virtual or face-to-face meetings, screen sharing allows all members to see the same materials from within the e-project. QDAS integration will always be stronger on research teams where you have senior researchers with good QDAS skills; likewise, integration may be limited on teams where only junior members possess strong QDAS skills. As QDAS use increases among researchers, perhaps we can look forward one day to a time when the presentation of the e-project itself will be as highly regarded as a peer-reviewed paper, dissertation, or book!

## Conclusion

Writing has a special relationship to qualitative research, a form of research deeply connected to the narrative. Our methodology is the communication of our process. Methodological in-process writing, whether it be in a log, memo, coding, or other form, is essential to the development of our approach to inquiry. These bits and pieces form the foundation of more formal methodological descriptions.

Formal methodological writing in qualitative research takes a wide range of forms. On a project of any sort, researchers are responsible for multiple varieties of the ideal methodological description. These descriptions are essential, but limited, compared to full formal methodological literature in which one pursues a methodological issue in depth.

As researchers become more familiar and skilled with QDAS, the e-project itself becomes a product of value, conveying methodological ideas as well as existing as an object to be admired for its own qualities.

Methodological reporting and topical or substantive reporting are always intertwined. One story cannot be told without the other. The communication of either is both informational and aesthetic. As an object of aesthetics, methodological reporting in its various forms is something to be critiqued, assessed, and admired for its own unique qualities.

## References

Altheide, David, and John Johnson. 1994. "Criteria for Assessing Interpretive Validity in Qualitative Research." In *Handbook of Qualitative Research*, edited by Norman K. Denzin and Yvonna S. Lincoln, 485–489. Thousand Oaks, CA: Sage Publications.

Davidson, Judith. 2000. *Living Reading: Exploring the Lives of Reading Teachers*. Edited by Joe L. Kincheloe and Shirley R. Steinberg. Vol. 124 of *Counterpoints: Studies in the Postmodern Theory of Education*. New York: Peter Lang.

Eisner, Elliot. 2007. "Alan 'Buddy' Peshkin." *Qualitative Research Journal* 6 (2): 99.

Emerson, Robert, Rachel Fretz, and Linda Shaw. 1995. *Writing Ethnographic Fieldnotes*. Chicago, IL: University of Chicago Press.

Harrison, Andrew J., Judith Davidson, Elizabeth Letourneau, Carl Paternite, and Karin Tusinski Miofsky. 2013. Building a Prevention Framework to

Address Teen "Sexting" Behaviors. Washington, D.C: U.S. Department of Justice.

Peshkin, Alan. 1991. *The Color of Strangers, the Color of Friends: The Play of Ethnicity in School and Community*. Chicago, IL: University of Chicago Press.

Peshkin, Alan. 1997. *Places of Memory: Whiteman's Schools and Native American Communities*. Edited by Joel Spring. 4 vols. Vol. 4 of *Sociocultural, Political, and Historical Studies in Education*. Mahwah, NJ: Lawrence Erlbaum Associates, Publishers.

Siltanen, Janet, Alette Willis, and Willow Scobie. 2008. "Separately Together: Working Reflexively as a Team." *International Journal of Social Research Methodology* 11 (1): 45–61. doi:10.1080/13645570701622116

Wolfe, Joanna. 2010. *Team Writing: A Guide to Working in Groups*. Boston, MA: Bedford/St. Martin's.

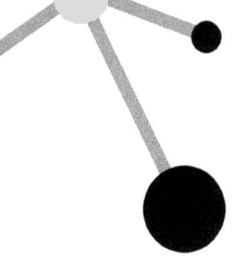

# 4

# SUBSTANTIVE WRITING IN TEAM-BASED QUALITATIVE RESEARCH

"SUBSTANTIVE WRITING" in this text refers to writing related to the substantive topic or question the team has pursued. Substantive writing comes into being through the interpretive processes of qualitative research.

As stated throughout this book, writing is the heart and soul of the qualitative research process. Informal writing is taking place at all times and as part of all stages of a qualitative research project. "Formal writing," meaning writing for public consumption, can occur at any place in the project process—from early on with a presentation on what you plan to do, to someplace in the middle where you present emerging findings, to looking back and learning what you have learned after the project has been completed.

In recent times, all areas of writing in qualitative research have faced significant challenges as researchers struggle to understand the theoretical implications of living in a post-modern and post-structural world. While many qualitative researchers are comfortable with their current expectations of the forms, processes, and standards for substantive writing that they produce, others are pushing the boundaries and taking exciting risks in regard to writing.

Teams offer special opportunities and challenges to the task of writing up the research, particularly substantive writing. Members' notions of what constitutes good or appropriate substantive writing forms may vary dramatically. Team members who push for experimentation with writing forms may be seen as being untrue to the scientific search for truth, or vice-versa. Like all other areas of team-based work, this area of writing can also be problematic unless approached with an open mind and respect.

As individuals or in groups, team members can take advantage of a variety of techniques to prompt their thinking in new ways as they work through the throes of interpretation, the stages they must walk through in order to reach a final product. In particular, while it may surprise those with a more scientific bent, arts-based research approaches offer many ways new perspectives can be developed among team members.

For teams developing their substantive writing, there are five components needing attention:

1. Interpretive work
2. Beginning the writing process
3. Testing for trustworthiness
4. Forms of reporting; kinds of writing
5. Insuring success

All components of these five elements do not necessarily follow each other in chronological order. Indeed, parts of each may occur simultaneously or in different order, depending upon the project.

## Interpretive Work

"Interpretive work" refers to the research activities that cross-cut layers of analysis to form substantive meaning in a qualitative research project. Many of the forms of interpretive work have parallels with the methodological *in process* tasks—from the organization of the database (and the creation of indices) to the writing of memos, and the development of intermediate and final forms of writing. There will be numerous intersections between substantive and methodological work, as the two are deeply intertwined with each other.

In chapters 2 and 3, there is information on several of the key processes that build the foundation for interpretive work (database development, memos, and various kinds of reviews). In this chapter,

I assume this knowledge as a foundation, and focus here more deeply on interpretive tasks that will help the researcher to write in a trustworthy way about the substantive findings of their work.

## Layering Interpretive Memos

Methodological memos have their parallel in interpretive work with the writing of memos about the propositions, claims, or hypotheses that are arising around the substantive focus of the project. If working in a digital tool, this interpretive work will begin with coding, creating definitions of codes, and linking items within and across documents. In other words, it will reflect the early processes in which the researcher is identifying patterns, noticing similarities and differences, and creating connections between the materials of the project and theories and their authors that exist outside of the project.

Small memos, perhaps a memo about a code or event that seems significant, make way for larger memos in which items are compared and patterns identified. Memos capture the questions, hypotheses, and propositions that researchers begin to formulate. Once articulated, these emerging notions become a focal point researchers can use to test the data. What can be considered an instance? What forms do these instances take? Can you find more instances of this idea? What is an illustration of this idea?

Over time, interpretive memos are lengthened or shortened as materials are connected and disconnected. Some ideas will flourish, and others will wither on the vine. Periodic pruning of the flora known as the qualitative research project is highly recommended, making for more vigorous growth!

These memos begin to form the materials that will become the substantive products of a project. The ideas and their connected pieces of data (evidence) are discussed in multiple groupings by the project team, in what I call interpretive meetings. These discussions allow for a new kind of discursive layering (and pruning) of the substantive material.

## Interpretive Meetings in Team-Based Research

Interpretive meetings, the real-space or virtual get-togethers where team members discuss interpretation of the collected data, are among the greatest moments of pure joy a qualitative researcher can experience. Members are saturated with the experience of the sites and participants, have cogitated on the possible meanings, and are bursting to share their ideas with each other. This potent mix usually leads to intense gatherings in which meanings and ideas can be identified, described, and contested. Naturally, assertions and explanations will need evidence and illustrations, and here the quality and organization of the database will be essential. The interpretive meeting is a core practice when working in the interpretive zone (Wasser & Bresler, 1996).

The process of meaning-making within a group requires intensive work among team members, which some have referred to as the "dialogic collaborative process" (Paulus, Woodside, & Ziegler, 2008). In an application of this model, Patterson, Hart, and Weaver (2010), in studying patients with mental delusions, found that this approach allowed for multilayered understanding of an elusive issue. They identified the importance of oral and written dialogue in the interpretive process.

Jarzabkowski, Bednarek, and Cabantous (2015), in describing the way their globally based ethnographic team collaborated to study the complicated topic of global reinsurance industry practices, identified five forms of sharing that developed trust and reinforced team cohesiveness as they also informed team members and extended interpretive work. "We engaged in five 'modes' of sharing in an effort to work through these challenges: emotional, thematic, analytic output, and codified sharing" (Jarzabkowski, Bednarek, & Cabantous, 2015. p. 19).

Thanks to the possibilities of the interpretive meeting, when it comes to unearthing rich findings, complex teams may have important advantages over individually conducted qualitative research. In particular, complex teams have many ways they can "work the boundaries" to create temporary disjuncture, useful to identifying and testing findings. By "working the boundaries," I refer to the capacity to juxtapose personal, professional, and other differences in useful ways. In the next section, I discuss some of the ways teams might plan to work the boundaries.

## Working the Boundaries

*Working the boundaries* is a critical interpretive tool for practitioners of qualitative research. It can be initiated from many different angles. It may be related to one's role or physical location on the project. It is often initiated by the contrasts between different disciplinary backgrounds. Recognizing positionality and subjectivity as they are embedded in age, gender, race, and ethnicity, among other autobiographical details, is essential to the task of using difference to deepen interpretative possibilities.

*Role or Location in Project*

When team members assemble to discuss the meaning of data collected, some of the first differences that might arise among members are in relationship to their role on the project. For instance, there may be differences between who is an on-the-ground collector of data and who is a more distanced reader. The people who were actually present when an interview was conducted may have a different understanding of the meaning than the team manager who is reading the interview transcripts without the benefit of having been present at the event. Discourse and negotiation are required to bring these views closer together and flesh out what was not said or noted in the field notes and to interpret the meaning of passages with multiple potential meanings.

Working across sites can surface unexpected differences among research participants. For instance, in the Sexting Project, we found a unique term—*flip*—used in the Southern regional site. African-American boys and girls used this term to describe the seduction of needy girls and their introduction into a circle of sexual activity with boys and men of the community. This term was not used by Caucasian people in the Southern regional site, nor by young people interviewed in the Northeast or Midwest. Only through comparison of field work across sites could the team make sense of this unique example (Davidson, 2014).

*Disciplines*

On any team, even the most seemingly homogeneous in composition, there will inevitably be individuals with different interests and strengths. Interdisciplinary teams take this one step further by specifically forming around the differences and intersections among disciplines. Different disciplines apply different lenses to looking at specific problems, including the application of different methods to the analysis of the issue. A sociologist will have different disciplinary skills and knowledge than an engineer or a medical doctor will. Using another example from the Sexting Project, the confluence of individuals with criminal justice, education, and social psychology backgrounds led to a series of conversations that shifted our original thinking about the role and meaning of sexting in teen's lives from an adult/prescriptive notion to a far more practice-based and youth-centered approach. Through working the boundaries among our disciplines, we came to replace the term "sexting" (an adult-conceived notion) with our notion of *the sexting continuum*, which described a spectrum of behavior from safe and trustworthy to unsafe, but with most of the activity in the middle around issues of teen sexual exploration that took place for a variety of reasons, from desire to belong, to a wish for affirmation and feedback about attractiveness (Harris & Davidson, 2014). This interpretation might not have come to be if we had not *worked the boundaries* of our project group.

By explicitly asking team members to react from their distinct disciplinary bases, group leaders can draw upon this specialized knowledge for use by the larger project.

### *Positionality, Subjectivity, or Autobiography: Age, Gender, Race, and Ethnicity*

Our "positionality," meaning the special characteristics that are ours alone as individual researchers, affords each of us a different view of the world. Members of a complex research team may be different in regard to age (20 vs. 40 vs. 60), gender orientation (male, female, gay, transgendered, or gender-neutral), race (Caucasian, African-American or Hispanic), or ethnicity (European, African, Asian, or Other), among a host of possible variables. In the social and historical settings of today, these differences may also indicate we possess significantly different experiences and attitudes. None of these attributes, however, should be conceived of as totally determining or monolithic.

In the process of forming a team, these differences should be probed, and they should also be returned to later as the interpretive process unfolds. By doing so, the team may uncover significant and important information that would not be available to a researcher operating without access to this circle of difference. Calling upon team members to reflect from their unique personal position provides new and different lenses on the data collected. While positionality may be a challenge, it is also a resource. For instance, women may interpret a situation described in field notes from a very different perspective than men, based upon their experience as a female gendered person in that situation. One gender may see threat in an action, whereas the other interprets the act as humor. Both views are needed for developing a full description.

In thinking about positionality, team members may also differ in their training in regard to formal theory about positionality, such as exposure to theories of colonialism, gender issues, or race-based relationships. These are very important theoretical lenses through which to consider the data collected. Again, ask members with special training to offer their viewpoints or assist with internal training needs. If there are no members with this kind of expertise, it may be useful to partner with individuals who do, or to access the services of a consultant. In particular, when addressing issues of positionality, it is important to test one's theories by using the emic or insider's views and the etic or outsider's views, in juxtaposition to each other.

## Make Strong Use of Consolidation and Visualization

Whether you are trying to make sense of a large or small amount of data, in either case, you will need to consolidate or synthesize the materials into categories that can be compared in different ways. Another term for "the consolidation of data" in qualitative research is "data reduction." Once data have been consolidated, reduced, or organized into meaningful categories, visualization can prove very important in helping researchers to distinguish the parts from the whole or to recognize what is foreground and what is background, or any other manner of patterning.

Qualitative researchers used visualization to aid analysis before digital tools were invented (Miles & Huberman, 1994; Strauss, 1987; MacQueen & Guest, 2008). They created tables and charts on blackboards and wrote notes that were tacked to bulletin boards, or drew on large pieces of paper. Digital tools like word processors, spreadsheets, and mind-mapping software continue this tradition into the digital age.

In a related development, today there is actually a surge of interest in the topic of visual notetaking that has had an impact in education (Davis, 2017), as well as on those who work with profit and nonprofit worlds (Smith, 2012). There are many useful methods and tools for incorporating visualization as part of the process of documentation and/or interpretation. Visualization processes can be conducted or displayed in hard copy or digitally.

I have long held that QDAS works naturally on the principles of consolidation and visualization (di Gregorio & Davidson, 2008). Coding creates labeled receptacles or filing drawers for storing items that can later be retrieved for group meetings—on or off line. Using a projector (for face-to-face meetings) or shared screen software (for online meetings), teams can view the ways the material has been organized and discuss the implications this has for analysis. Comparing and discussing relationships among codes forces researchers to think about the synthesis of the materials. Modeling tools, which are generally part of QDAS packages now, extend the ability to work with the condensed form of an idea (a code is an example of a condensed form) to develop pictures of consolidated data. Through hyperlinking, these tools also allow a reader to enter the detailed materials behind the codes.

Using the Sexting Project as an example, our research team contained members who were strong users of the QDAS package NVivo, as well as non-users. However, all members, regardless of their NVivo access or skill level, could make use of the visualization capacities through viewing screenshots of the materials organized within NVivo. These screenshots depicted key ideas represented by the use of coding, linking, searching, and modeling tools and could be shared online and face-to-face. While a small group of strong users worked with the tool in one way, the larger group had punctuated use of the e-project, particularly in the context of what we referred to as "interpretive meetings." Documentation of this interpretive work led to emergence of critical themes, identification of findings, and subsequent writing that fixed our ideas (Davidson, Thompson, & Harris, 2017).

## Beginning the Writing Process: From Parallel Play to Collaborative Writing

Increasingly on my campus, and I am sure on others, researchers join forces to write together in a form of parallel play. We simply come together at the same time and place—and write. We do it because it works—it makes us accountable and productive. We turn off the outside world and stay focused on the writing we need to do. Sitting silently side by side, sometimes for hours, we work on different projects while we take comfort in our shared presence.

Parallel play is one end of the spectrum of joint writing, but there are numerous places along the spectrum of joint writing where researchers assemble for writing activities. Moreover, you can move up and down along the spectrum, shifting position as it makes sense for your needs and the tasks at hand.

There are numerous strategies a team can make use of to support the full spectrum of collaborative writing. Some of these are:

*Shared writing times:* Schedule a weekly time for members to come together and write. These may be devoted to a collaborative endeavor or simply for individual writing time.

*Writing workshops:* Schedule writing workshops for team members (online or off) to focus on a particular piece of writing or to learn specific techniques. Working with a writing expert can move everyone forward.

*Writing retreats:* A different and relaxing location can help to revive the creative juices. Make dedicated time to write away from your usual workplace where you can meet with others or be alone to work on your writing. Work bars, which are springing up in many cities, are designed for just such activities, but there are other possibilities as well.

*Online writing coaching or daily check-ins:* There are many online writing support programs where you post your daily writing achievements and get encouragement from the coach and others in your small group. This can be very effective for establishing daily writing habits. An online group of this sort could be set up with the explicit purpose of meeting the needs of a specific team.

*Writing consultants or productivity coaches:* Writing consultants or productivity coaches can be brought in to study your group processes and help team members develop more efficient strategies, particularly around planning and executing writing tasks. Sometimes it is very helpful to have an outside eye and someone with new information to help move the group ahead with their tasks.

Writing together can have its share of challenges, particularly if group members do not take time to create shared understandings around writing goals, processes, and procedures. Personal differences in personality, culture, gender, and style can support or challenge the writing process. Setting out clear expectations at the beginning can help to make any group function better (Wolfe, 2010).

When team leaders assist their group members to learn more about writing and become more skilled and productive in regard to writing, they are providing them with skills for life that transcend all fields. Supporting professional development in the area of writing is an important way by which leaders can encourage team members in their careers.

## Testing Trustworthiness: Findings and Results

In social science terms, a finding or result signifies a nugget, a fact, something that is known (positive or negative) or agreed upon about the topic under consideration. This nugget invariably started out as a hypothesis or proposition, but now it is a finding or result, because the authors believe they can support the assertion with data, collected and analyzed in the course of the project.

For team members, the next key question is: Did we get it right? In other words, what claims can we make for the validity or trustworthiness of our results? Project members know that this will be the deciding factor when the work goes public. So before the moment of publication, they do everything possible to ensure their work meets a standard of truth commensurate with the epistemological positions in which they are embedded.

Arguments about trustworthiness in qualitative research are complex. As a basic starting point for the average team, I would suggest a standard that borrows heavily from Maxwell's notions of trustworthiness (Maxwell, 1996), with strong additions of ideas about theory and symbolization in interpretation (Geertz, 1973), and a good dose of healthy skepticism of the critical-theory sort (Dutta, 2014).

Three arenas to probe in search of trustworthiness:

**Descriptive**—What happened? Does everyone agree to the description?
**Interpretive**—What does it mean? What connections to larger notions of theory and symbolization are now understood?

**Critical**—Whom does it affect and how? What is the impact? How is power present? What are the asymmetries in the exercise of power? In particular, how are we, the researchers, complicit in regimes of power related to this issue?

In regard to writing up the results of a study, regardless if they are presented in standardized or non-standardized form, it is important to give the reader a sense of the warrants of truth put forward by the authors and the attention that was paid to questioning the results. "We all agreed" is not good enough. The reader needs to know how the team used the multiple perspectives of the team to test the results, reviewed and tested the idea through examination of the data, and compared the ideas to the views of substantive literature on same or related topics.

## Rewriting Research Roles: Participants as Collaborators

Increasingly, researchers are moving away from colonial era models of researcher vs researchee to a model of hybrid roles and participation in which participants are more than merely instrumental, but fellow humans and collaborators in knowledge creation. This shift has important implications for individual researchers and those engaging in team research, as it signals a change in both form and perspective (Fielding, 2012). In regard to writing up research produced by teams, attention must now be given to sharing authorship roles with participants, providing different forms of credit, and, of greatest importance, demonstrating partnership with, rather than power over, researchees (Dutta, 2014, 2016).

As this shift is implemented, there are increasing numbers of research products that can serve as examples for how this can be done. These examples light the way for others, opening new territory for the writing up of results that have been reached in democratic, collaborative, and mutually respectful ways.

## Forms of Reporting: Kinds of Writing

This section of the chapter focuses on two related issues in regard to substantive writing in qualitative research: (1) What might you report; and (2) What form can that report take?

## What Might You Report?

While substantive writing can take many different forms, for the most part regardless of the form, a report will focus on one of these four choices.

1. Report on the overall project and the breadth of findings:

   The first form of reporting describes or attends to the project as a whole. This is an umbrella view of the project and its overall findings.

2. Report on selected findings of the project:

   A report on selected findings will provide overall information about the project (question, scope, methods, etc.), but will present specific finding(s) for deeper discussion.

3. Report focusing on anomalies (presence/absence—odditiesquestions—the cases of one):

   In every project undertaken, there are anomalies, things that can't be fitted into the normal range of explanation. There are unexpected things that are present, or there are expected things that are absent. Anomalies are worthy of reporting for their own sake.

4. Discussions of implications or recommendations:

   For every project, there is the issue of implications. In other words, what should we do about this? If we know this, what can we assume might follow from this? Or what are the next steps that should be taken? This is the arena of recommendations.

Depending upon the form in which the report is presented—standardized social science writing, or a non-standardized or more creative format—the impact on the reader/viewer can be vastly different. Consideration of audience and form, then, becomes highly significant.

## What Forms Can Your Reporting Take?

There are two major categories the written products of complex teams will fall into: standardized social science writing or creative social science writing. Both of these approaches are distinct, but there are many points of hybridization across genre, and hybridization is definitely on the rise.

## Standardized Social Science Writing and Presentation

Standardized social science writing relies on the scientific model of research presentation, adapted to the form of qualitative research. The introduction of such a piece begins with a discussion of the problem, which segues to identification of a need, followed by a declaration of the research question. This background section is followed by a description of the methodology (where criteria for validity or trustworthiness may also be addressed), a section in which findings are described, followed by a discussion section, and a conclusion. This formulaic approach is consistent and easy to follow for either a reader or writer.

Individual presses, journal publishers, or others who serve as the gatekeepers for social science publication generally specify a required style for the materials they will accept, such as the American Psychological Association (APA), Modern Language Association (MLA), or Associated Press (AP). These organizations publish stylebooks that describe the rules a writer must follow when producing an article, paper, or book in that style (Table 4.1).

Not all qualitative research, whether individual or team-based, is conducted by academics. However, for those in academia, publishing in peer-reviewed journals with high impact factors is essential to one's career. In a peer-reviewed journal process, it is one's academic peers, or experts in related work, who make the decision about the worth of one's writing. In thinking about publishing monographs or books, the reputation of the press and whether or not it uses a peer-reviewed process will also figure in decisions about where to publish.

In regard to non–peer-reviewed publication opportunities, some products are required of the project. As an example, government agencies or other private funders require reports from their grantees, and they will usually stipulate the form in which the report must be presented.

Larger research teams usually mean outside funding, which is almost always coupled with a greater responsibility to report to that funder and disseminate results in a timely way in order to justify spending. Larger teams with more specified reporting

Table 4.1
**Examples of Forms of Standardized Social Science Writing and Presentation**

| Peer-Reviewed | Non–Peer-Reviewed |
|---|---|
| Presentations at academic conferences | Reports to funders or oversight bodies |
| Scholarly journal articles: Class peer-reviewed journal articles | General-interest publications |
| Book products; monographs, series, full volumes; scholarly press and peer-review process | Public dissemination, including such outlets as newspapers or other digital news sources |
| Textbooks: Designed to described consolidated or accepted points within the field. Publisher may or may not use a formal peer-reviewed process | Invited presentations to specific audiences |
| Encyclopedias: Designed to provide short informative materials—treatment falls between textbook (expanded) and dictionary (brief) Generally written by a subject area expert or someone relying on expert materials | |

responsibilities may also bring with them a more hierarchical approach to writing responsibilities. Reports to funders are a key responsibility of the principal investigator (PI), although they may be written largely or in part by others, as the PI is the legally responsible party.

There is also a range of other dissemination outlets that are also non–peer-reviewed—from newspapers and magazines, to some textbooks or other web publications. These may be important places to tell the story of the project and may well garner a much larger audience for the work than narrower scholarly locations.

### Non-Standardized Writing or Creative Writing in the Social Sciences

Non-standardized or creative writing in the social sciences has come about as a result of several factors, including the rise of arts-based research approaches, new digital forms of publication, and the changing relationships among researchers and researchees.

Whereas standardized forms of social science writing are extremely formulaic, non-standardized writing is not. In the last several years, a number of guides for writing outside of the standardized model have emerged (Caulley, 2008; Goodall, 2000, 2008). Examples of creative forms of social science writing influenced by arts-based research include autoethnography, ethnopoetics, performance ethnography, and art exhibits to social fiction and creative nonfiction. They may also be couched in forms that have become familiar to us from our use of digital media, including blogs, Twitter, Facebook, Instagram, and Wikipedia entries, as well as podcasts, vodcasts, and such outlets as YouTube and Vimeo. Other products are instructionally derived, such as Massive Open Online Courses (MOOKS). Increasingly, researchers are now experimenting with such adaptable forms as applications (or apps).

Even for those who don't feel comfortable presenting their findings in these forms, there are many techniques embedded in the production of these new forms that can serve as models for new ways of reinvigorating the writing process of standardized social science writing. I present a handful of examples of creative nonfiction approaches with the hope that readers will take it upon themselves to explore this area in greater depth.

## Creative Nonfiction

In seeking to enliven their writing, qualitative researchers have turned to the emerging field of creative nonfiction; that is, nonfiction writing that draws upon techniques that had previously been exclusively the domain of fiction—poetry, novels, and short stories (Caulley, 2007, 2008). In the 2000s, texts begin to emerge that talked the timid qualitative researcher through techniques for making this dramatic shift (Goodall, 2008, 2000).

Fast forward to today, when social scientists have come to accept these ideas and are hungry to learn these techniques. At my institution, the University of Massachusetts–Lowell, the Center for Women and Work and the Qualitative Research Network sponsored a very well attended day-long faculty workshop by a colleague from our English Department, nationally recognized creative nonfiction writer Maureen Stanton. Stanton is the author of, among other titles, *Killer Stuff and Tons of Money: An Insider's Look at the World of Flea Markets, Antiques, and Collecting* (Stanton, 2011). To our eager group, Stanton provided explicit creative nonfiction techniques that could be applied to support social science writing and let us spend time practicing the various ones she presented, such as fleshing out a character, presenting the details of a setting, or adding dialogue. These techniques provided new ways to write better and more interesting social science, whether one was aiming for an experimental presentation or a more conservative one.

Complex teams present the perfect conditions for writing workshops that can make use of these approaches. There are multiple members who are knowledgeable about the same or similar data, and connected through diverse communication channels. Moreover, these groups have already done the significant hard work to develop trust that will allow for this sort of risk-taking. In qualitative research, it is actually surprising that we don't have more information about the ways such teams write and the experiments that have been made using the team as a base for homegrown writing workshops.

### Social Fiction

Social fiction is an arena in which researchers from diverse fields are making publication inroads, including qualitative researchers. Sociologist Patricia Leavy launched her social fiction series through Sense Publications. Each fiction volume is written by a researcher with significant research experience in the topic presented. The issues addressed range from eating disorders and sexuality to the complexities of teaching and racism. Each volume in the series provides good writing, emotionally compelling plots, and strong detailed information on a specific social science topic, conveyed in an interesting and lively format. Leavy demonstrates that qualitative research can be presented as fiction, not just nonfiction, and in doing so, can reach new and wider audiences than traditional reports.

Given the genesis of many complex research teams (funded research, conservative environment), presenting the findings of the work as fiction may not be an option, but there are many techniques of fiction, such as the development of characters, the use of dialogue, or the writing of rich descriptions, that can provide interest to nonfiction pieces. Also, fictional techniques may provide creative means of developing knowledge and ideas prior to the final development of a nonfiction piece, as a kind of interpretive exercise. This is definitely within the realm we now refer to as creative nonfiction.

## Autoethnography

An important starting point for the arts-based research movement in qualitative research was Carolyn Ellis's pioneering work in "autoethnography," a form of qualitative research in which autobiography is integrated with ethnography (Ellis, 2004). Ellis blended this form with social fiction to create *The Ethnographic I: A Methodological Novel About Autoethnography*, a novel about a qualitative research instructor teaching a class in autoethnography.

The response to Ellis's declaration of the form has been remarkable. Bochner and Ellis (2016) report that in 1999, there were fewer than 50 articles accessible on the topic through electronic searches, but by 2014, that number had grown to 17,000. Moreover, they claim that 50% of the presentations today at the International Congress of Qualitative Inquiry (ICQI) are now some form of autoethnography.

Autoethnography builds in many ways on what was already an important discussion in qualitative research regarding the topic of subjectivity (Peshkin, 1997, 1991; Phillips, 1990; Davidson, 2012). The result of this convergence of ideas is that regardless of your stance on qualitative research (realist or constructivist), it has become a necessity among qualitative researchers to probe or write about their subjectivity in relationship to the topic of study.

For researchers working on complex teams, autobiographic conversations will be part of team-formation, and autobiographical details will be referred to throughout interpretive discussions as the group tries to probe findings and reactions of its members. Extending the opportunity to write about individual members' interests and experiences in relationship to the topic under study often unearths important perspectives or new resources that can contribute to the group's work. In particular, autobiographical writing can be useful for cross-cultural groups, providing a means of establishing the multiple caches of expertise present in the group and making their contents explicit.

## Arts-Based Techniques for Interrogating Meaning

Interrogating for meaning is a central process of interpretation in qualitative research. We do this by any means possible, from fracturing and indexing to juxtaposing, and auditioning through the curation of different collections of data.

Following, I list some examples of arts-based techniques that can be used for interrogating meaning from the materials and experiences collected by team members. This is only a handful of the possibilities available, but I hope they will pique your interest to explore this area in greater depth.

*Poetry: Found and Responsive* Poetry can serve many ends in the process of interrogating for meaning. **Found poetry** is sometimes a useful place to start. Identify an interesting passage of data, extract, and arrange the passage in a poetic manner that allows you to play with different potential meanings. You will be surprised to learn how reading the lines with different pauses or emphases helps you to see new possibilities. New formatting to visually move lines into different places on a page can also create new possibilities of meaning.

At another time, a useful way of using poetry is through **responsive poetry**. Identify a place of interest in the data—an event or experience, a participant, a place—whatever holds interest. Write a poem that expresses the feelings or evocation you associate with it. Use this poem as a lens for deepening the understanding you bring to the data (Faulkner, 2009).

*Drama: Verbatim and Performative Ethnography* Like poetry, drama has also been repurposed for the needs of qualitative researchers, and performative ethnography can take many forms in regard to process and product. For instance, it may be a formal script developed by the researcher based upon ideas drawn from a research project, or it could be staged as a series of improvisations (Pellias, 2008; Denzin, 2003; Saldana, 2008; Hamera, 2011).

In the "Through Their Eyes Project" that I developed on my campus, graduate students interrogated undergraduates from two first-year writing courses about the transitional challenges of entering higher education. Subsequently, a doctoral student used these verbatim interview transcripts to develop a script formed from quotations that discussed the key issues undergraduates raised in the interviews. These materials served as the basis for a multimedia video production of a drama developed from the data that was acted out by high school students from a local district and filmed by that town's local cable channel (Davidson, 2017; Davidson, Whittlesey, & Bresler, 2017).

*Image/Object to Write* This is the name I have given to a group of techniques that exist at a point between the verbal and visual or material, in which a visual depiction or material object serves as the prompt for writing. For instance, a photograph(s) of a research site or activities related to the research project can serve as the beginning point for written reflections by team members. Description of the place or event and its context within the practice of project participants can be a starting point for extended writing about the meanings embedded in the view presented by the photograph(s) (Collier & Collier, 1986; Pink, 2001).

Bresler (2013) describes how the visual arts (through an art museum visit) can be used to explore qualitative research processes and to assist students to heighten their awareness of methodological issues.

Sensory Ethnography

Many years ago, my qualitative research class undertook an experiment in sensory ethnography, each member providing the class with a sense of the sounds they noticed in their fieldwork. One student, a labor activist working on a large construction site, made the repetitive sounds of huge digging machines. We were immediately conveyed to the noisy world where she was spending her days. Her sounds gave those of us in the class a visceral experience of what it was like to do fieldwork in that dangerous, clanging, and honking world, where hardhats were required.

Attention to the sensory in qualitative research has been slow to grow, but once experienced cannot be denied. Exploring the sensory components of a fieldwork experience can help to elicit details that might have been overlooked. It will also provide fieldworkers and others with more direct paths into the feelings and perspectives of research participants (Pink, 2015).

In most qualitative work, words (oral, spoken or written language) get the most attention, followed by selected visual components, and much later down the line come sounds. This hierarchy of sensory attention privileges the academic in many ways, but may not be true to the experiences of people from non-academic or non-literate worlds.

## Conditions to Ensure Success

Many researchers, qualitative included, may not feel comfortable heading out into the new territory of non-standardized social science writing. In their eyes, it may lack scientific reliability; or, not having worked with the arts since childhood, it may be far too unfamiliar. Regardless, all can do it, and all can benefit. Once they try it, many will be surprised at the insight it brings. High technical skill is not required, because you are not seeking to create a dramatic or visual masterpiece. Rather, you are searching out new means of encountering the data and ideas—visualization, making, literary forms—all can be useful in bringing out hidden perspectives, creating new juxtapositions, and developing new linkages.

Particularly important is the talk around the form you try. Trying to describe it, discussing your process, listening to others do the same, these bring new layers of text to interpretation and often uncover ideas you did not know you possessed. The most creative approaches, however, will be for naught without the conditions that will ensure full processing and development of final written products.

## Goals, Responsibilities, and Timelines

One of the most important issues in regard to collaborative writing is the establishment of goals, responsibilities, and timelines. These things cannot be left to chance or happenstance. The work will not be completed without this planning.

Three questions guide these tasks:

1. What do we want to accomplish?
2. Who will do what?
3. When is it due?

At the highest level, "accomplishment" in this realm refers to the audiences you wish to inform, the forms of writing that will serve as the best vehicles for your message, and the kinds of media in which you seek publication. At a more specific level, the team will want to determine what aspects of the project or findings they wish to address and how this can be done.

One of the positives of working on a multi-member team is that there are more individuals among whom the work can be spread. It is important to make sure that the broadest number of people on the team get to participate in some form on the writing projects, making contributions appropriate to their role and skills and acknowledging their participation in an appropriate manner. It's also important to be clear about who is doing what. Doing these things will help to extend a sense of empowerment to each team member, and thus build higher morale among team members.

A complex team cannot get the work accomplished without due dates and holding members accountable for the tasks they have promised to deliver. Ironically, many complex project teams stay very much on task and on schedule through planning, data collection, and coding, but as they head toward writing, they spin off the track, and the production of written materials cannot be accomplished. This is sad because it means the collective wisdom of the project is never shared to the extent that it could be.

There are important tools that can help with establishing goals, responsibilities, and timelines, but until recently, many project leaders in social science research fields were not as aware of them as they might have been. These include Gantt charts, Kanban tools, and other planning boards such as the digital tool Trello. These are referred to in Chapter 1 as part of the discussion on the digital toolkit a team will need. While these planning tools can be used in hard copy, for multi-sited and dispersed teams it is better to use cloud-based tools where members have access from anywhere in the world.

As you reach the end of the writing process, you will probably move into a formal writing process tool where editing software makes writing tasks manageable. You will also want to store carefully labeled copies in jointly shared digital work areas where all writers have access, can make contributions, and read the different editions as they are completed.

## Who Will Get Credit for What?

This discussion was raised in Chapter 2 of this book. I return to it frequently as a reminder and to underscore the point that credit—meaning authorship, acknowledgements, or other formal reference to those who have participated directly or indirectly in the development of the product—is very important, particularly in academia or related areas of work where it serves as one of the key signifiers of professional recognition. A reminder about credit is also important in the discussion on substantive writing, in that these products are the ones that will weigh most significantly for individuals, their institutions, and the disciplines to which they belong.

Life will be much easier for everyone on the team if discussions about how credit will be distributed take place early on in the process. Moreover, the criteria for how credit is distributed should be as transparent as possible to all team members. Allocation of credit should be fair and discussed in a transparent manner.

Standard forms of social science writing offer credit in the form of: first author, second author and more, acknowledgements, and references.

Non-standard or creative forms of social science may list different roles in regard to the distribution of credit, such as producer, director, camera person, or poet. For instance, one product that emerged from the "Through Their Eyes" project described earlier in this chapter was a video. When we got to the credits for the actual video, creativity was needed to describe the roles. As leader of the project, I was dubbed the "executive producer"; the doctoral student who was writer and organizer was titled "Director"; and the undergraduate student who had assisted on many parts of the work was given the role of "Assistant and Grip" (Davidson, Whittlesey, & Bresler, 2017; Davidson, 2017). This format recognized academic standards (the faculty advisor is responsible for student work) and community expectations for film credits (role of producer, director, assistant and grip).

Regardless of the form of the product—standardized or creative—team members feel slighted if one member of the group is receiving credit for work they did not do, just as they also feel slighted when a member does not receive credit for the work to which they contributed. In either case, justice is not served, and the negative effects can linger long beyond the end of the project.

The discussion of credit is a matter that refers to those who are internal to the project, as well as those who are external to it. Externally, individuals often contribute to the project through the professional literature they have produced. Referencing the work that has helped to shape the ideas presented becomes more complicated with team projects, so it is important to ensure all appropriate team members review the materials and provide the references that were significant in their discipline or thinking related to the topic. In terms of the development of ideas, we are always indebted to others. In addition, readers are assisted by appropriate references, as it allows them to see the pathway authors have taken to get to their ideas. Your final products are not the place for payback for slights in your professional life, and it is always better to take the high road when acknowledging others' assistance or lack thereof.

## Conclusion

Writing about the substance of a research project is the *raison d'être* of most researchers. There are widening writing possibilities available to researchers today, and as a result, a broader number of forms that the writing up of results can take. These changes in perspectives on writing have implications for the products of writing work, but also for the process and production of writing.

Team research offers members wonderful opportunities for collaborative writing, growth, and development that are not always available to the individual researcher pursing a project alone. The resources of the team can promote good things for all writers. These possibilities, however, require giving attention to mundane, but important tasks, such as goals, responsibility, and deadline setting; establishing the use of appropriate technologies to support writing, and ensuring that interpretive work gets adequate time.

An important trend in research is the movement toward greater partnership with participants, and this shift is also changing expectations in writing. For multi-member, multi-site studies, such shifts will require training in new perspectives and exposure to examples of the forms collaborative products can take when research participants are included in new ways.

This is an exciting moment in regard to the progress of writing in the social sciences. It remains to be seen where our history and the emerging trends will take us as writers.

## References

Bochner, Arthur, and Carolyn Ellis. 2016. "The ICQI and the Rise of Autoethnography: Solidarity Through Community." *International Review of Qualitative Research* 9 (2): 208–217. doi:10.1525/irqr2016.9.2.208.

Bresler, Liora. 2013. "Experiential Pedagogies in Research Education: Drawing on Engagement with Artworks." In *Teaching and Learning Emergent Research Methodologies in Art Education*, edited by C. Stout, 43–63. Reston, VA: National Art Education Association.

Caulley, Darrel N. 2007. "Doing and Writing Qualitative Research." *Qualitative Research Journal* 2 (2): 105.

Caulley, Darrel N. 2008. "Making Qualitative Research Reports Less Boring: The Techniques of Writing Creative Nonfiction." *Qualitative Inquiry* 14 (3): 424–449. doi:10.1177/1077800407311961.

Collier, John, Jr., and Malcolm Collier. 1986. *Visual Anthropology: Photography as a Research Method*. Albuquerque, NM: University of New Mexico Press.

Davidson, J. 2017. "'Through Their Eyes': Understanding Retention in Higher Education Through a Multi-partner Research Project on Transitional Challenges Facing Incoming Undergraduates." Panel presentation. Portsmouth, NH: New England Educational Research Association.

Davidson, Judith. 2012. "The Journal Project and the I in Qualitative Research: Three Theoretical Lenses on Subjectivity and Self." *The Qualitative Report* 17 (32): 1–13. Retrieved from https://nsuworks.nova.edu/tqr/vol17/iss32/1.

Davidson, Judith. 2014. *Sexting: Gender and Teens*, edited by Patricia Leavy. Vol. 3, *Teaching Gender*. Rotterdam, Netherlands: Sense Publications.

Davidson, Judith, Shanna Rose Thompson, and Andrew J. Harris. 2017. "Qualitative Data Analysis Software Practices in Complex Research Teams: Troubling the Assumptions About Transparency and Portability." *Qualitative Inquiry* 23 (10): 779–788. doi:10.1177/1077800417731082.

Davidson, Judith, Christine Whittlesey, and Liora Bresler. 2017. "Performance Ethnography as Qualitative Inquiry in the Public Sphere." International Congress of Qualitative Inquiry, University of Illinois, Urbana–Champaign, Illinois.

Davis, Vicky. 2017. "Notetaking Skills for 21st Century Students." *Coolcat Teacher*, Aug. 15, 2017. http://www.coolcatteacher.com/note-taking-skills-21st-century-students/.

Denzin, Norman K. 2003. *Performance Ethnography: Critical Pedagogy and the Politics of Culture*. Thousand Oaks, CA: Sage Publications.

di Gregorio, Silvana, and Judith Davidson. 2008. *Qualitative Research Design for Software Users*. Milton Keynes, UK: McGraw-Hill Education.

Dutta, Urmitapa. 2014. "Critical Ethnography." In *Qualitative Methodologies: A Practical Guide*, edited by Jane Mills and Melanie Birks, 89–105. London: Sage Publications.

Dutta, Urmitapa. 2016. "Ethnographic Approaches." In *Handbook of Methodological Approaches to Community-Based Research: Qualitative,*

*Quantitative, and Mixed Methods*, edited by Leonard Jason and David Glenwick, 69–79. Oxford, UK: Oxford University Press.

Ellis, Carolyn. 2004. *The Ethnographic I: A Methodological Novel About Autoethnography*, edited by Carolyn Ellis and Arthur Bochner. 16 vols. Vol. 13, *Ethnographic Alternatives*. Walnut Creek, CA: Altamira Press.

Faulkner, Sandra. 2009. *Poetry as Method: Reporting Research Through Verse*. Walnut Creek, CA: Left Coast Press.

Fielding, Nigel G. 2012. "The Diverse Worlds and Research Practices of Qualitative Software." *Forum: Qualitative Social Research* 13 (2): 1–18.

Geertz, Clifford. 1973. *The Interpretation of Cultures: Selected Essays by Clifford Geertz*. New York: Basic Books.

Goodall, H. L. (Bud) Jr. 2000. *Writing the New Ethnography*, edited by Carolyn Ellis and Arthur Bochner. 7 vols. Vol. 7, *Ethnographic Alternatives Book Series*. Walnut Creek, CA: Altamira Press.

Goodall, H. L. (Bud) Jr. 2008. *Writing Qualitative Inquiry: Self, Stories, and Academic Life*. Edited by Arthur Bochner and Carolyn Ellis. 6 vols. Vol. 6, *Writing Lives: Ethnographic Narratives*. Walnut Creek, CA: Left Coast Press.

Hamera, Judith. 2011. "Performance Ethnography." In *The Sage Handbook of Qualitative Research*, edited by Norman K. Denzin and Yvonna S. Lincoln, 317–329. Thousand Oaks, CA: Sage Publications.

Harris, Andrew J., and Judith Davidson. 2014. "Lessons for Youth Professionals from the Sexting Project." Practitioner Conference of the Middlesex District Attorney's Office, University of Massachusetts–Lowell, March 21, 2014.

Jarzabkowski, Paula, Rebecca Bednarek, and Laure Cabantous. 2015. "Conducting Global Team-Based Ethnography: Methodological Challenges and Practical Methods." *Human Relations* 68 (1): 3.

MacQueen, Kathleen M., and Greg Guest. 2008. *Handbook for Team-Based Qualitative Research*. Lanham, MD: Altamira Press.

Maxwell, Joseph A. 1996. *Qualitative Research Design: An Interactive Approach*. Thousand Oaks, CA: Sage Publications.

Miles, Matthew B., and A. Michael Huberman. 1994. *An Expanded Sourcebook: Qualitative Data Analysis*. 2nd ed. Thousand Oaks, CA: Sage Publications.

Patterson, Sue E., Jozella Hart, Tim D. Weaver. 2010. "Delusions and Qualitative Confusions: A Dialogic Collaborative Exploration." *Qualitative Health Research* 20 (7): 1008.

Paulus, Trena, Marianne Woodside, and Mary Ziegler. 2008. "Extending the Conversation: Qualitative Research as Dialogic Collaborative Process." *The Qualitative Report* 13 (2): 226–243. Retrieved from https://nsuworks.nova.edu/tqr/vol13/iss2/6.

Pellias, Ronald J. 2008. "Performative Inquiry: Embodiment and Its Challenges." In *Handbook of the Arts in Qualitative Research: Perspectives, Methodologies, Examples, and Issues*, edited by J. Gary Knowles and Ardra Cole, 185–193. Thousand Oaks, CA: Sage Publications.

Peshkin, Alan. 1991. *The Color of Strangers, the Color of Friends: The Play of Ethnicity in School and Community*. Chicago, IL: University of Chicago Press.

Peshkin, Alan. 1997. *Places of Memory: Whiteman's Schools and Native American Communities*, edited by Joel Spring. 4 vols. Vol. 4, *Sociocultural, Political, and Historical Studies in Education*. Mahwah, NJ: Lawrence Erlbaum Associates, Publishers.

Phillips, D. C. 1990. "Subjectivity and Objectivity: An Objective Inquiry." In *Qualitative Inquiry in Education: The Continuing Debate*, edited by Elliot Eisner and Alan Peshkin, 19–37. New York: Teachers College Press.

Pink, S. 2015. *Doing Sensory Ethnography*. London: Sage Publications.

Pink, Sarah. 2001. *Doing Visual Ethnography*. London: Sage Publications.

Saldana, Johnny. 2008. "Ethnodrama and Ethnotheatre." In *Handbook of the Arts in Qualitative Research: Perspectives, Methodologies, Examples, and Issues*, edited by J. Gary Knowles and Ardra Cole, 195–207. Thousand Oaks, CA: Sage Publications.

Smith, Rachel. 2012. "TedxUFM." In *Drawing in Class*, edited by Rachel Smith. Retrieved from http://digitalfacilitation.net/.

Stanton, Maureen. 2011. *Killer Stuff and Tons of Money: An Insider's Look at the World of Flea Markets, Antiques, and Collecting*. London: Penguin Publishers.

Strauss, Anselm L. 1987. *Qualitative Analysis for Social Scientists*. Cambridge, UK: Cambridge University Press.

Wasser, Judith Davidson, and Liora Bresler. 1996. "Working in the Interpretive Zone: Conceptualizing Collaboration in Qualitative Research Teams." *Educational Researcher* 25 (5): 5–15.

Wolfe, Joanna. 2010. *Team Writing: A Guide to Working in Groups*. Boston, MA: Bedford/St. Martin's.

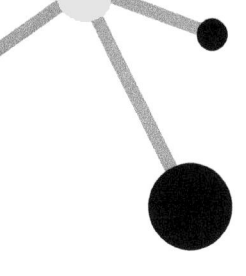

# 5

# TRENDS, ISSUES, AND CONSIDERATIONS

IN THIS final chapter, I turn my sights to the trends, issues, and considerations that face us in the future and that qualitative researchers must attend to if they are to be successful on team-based endeavors. This book, like all books, appears at a particular point on an imaginary timeline of human activity. As soon as it appears, it is surpassed by the forward march of time, making its context and perspective a thing of the past. For that reason, it is helpful at the end to try to imagine what is coming—to make predictions and to provide suggestions based on those predictions. Here, as in the earlier chapters, my focus is on the role of writing in team-based qualitative research.

In this chapter, I discuss the **trends** I can predict will be of importance to qualitative researchers and their team-based work; I consider **issues** on the horizon and heading quickly toward us; and, I reflect upon **considerations** needing responses if we are to move forward doing this kind of work—team-based qualitative research work.

## Trends I Can Predict

In regard to the practice of team-based qualitative research, here are three significant trends I predict will continue:

### Team-Based Research Projects, Particularly Mixed-Methods Studies, Will Continue to Increase in Importance and Diversity, Enfolding Qualitative Methods Within Their Arms

Whether you work in universities or outside of higher education in government, non-governmental or commercial organizations, studies are becoming more problem-based and less methodologically restricted. By this I mean, as Leavy (2011) describes in her work on transdisciplinary approaches, that answering the question or solving the problem will take precedence over methodological purity. You will do what it takes. Sometimes that will mean numbers, and sometimes narratives, and most often it will require people with skill in both. We will still need methodological specialists, but these specialists will have more opportunity to mix with each other, developing new ways of understanding mixed and non-mixed methodologies. Team-based projects will be increasingly interdisciplinary and global in perspective and membership.

It also is my prediction that not only will team-based research projects increase in number, but these teams will also be more and more interdisciplinary and global. In a global world facing large interconnected problems where research is problem-focused, diverse disciplines will necessarily be pressed into service. Working within a single discipline may or may not require a team-based approach, but working across disciplines most certainly requires team-based approaches.

Moreover, while a given study may be focused on a particular locality, the interconnected nature of the problems or issues human beings face on our planet will lead to global considerations, if not global partners, in thinking about the issues. Team-based projects will make increasingly strong use of digital tools in all aspects of their work.

As research tasks become more complicated, as they do with team-based research, digital tools will be called into action. To date, qualitative data analysis tools (QDAS) have served as an anchor software for qualitative researchers, providing them with a digital space and tools unique to the undertaking of this form of research. For some high-end QDAS users, the "e-project," meaning the digital container QDAS provides for project materials, is evolving into its own form of publication genre, in which data collection, analysis, and representation are combined in one location (di Gregorio & Davidson, 2008; Davidson, 2005).

While QDAS will most certainly play an important role, there are many other digital tools team-based qualitative researchers will need to make use of, including such items as digital clipping tools, digital notebooks, Reference Managers, project planning software, and mobile apps. In our rapidly evolving digital society, new digital tools with application for research are popping up daily (Paulus, Lester, & Dempster, 2014).

As the digital increasingly becomes the normal mode, the creation of digital tools becomes simplified, and increasingly we can assume not only that tool construction will be the province of software developers, but that qualitative researchers will take charge of their own digital tool development (Do & Yamagata-Lynch, 2017).

## Big Data Will Continue as a World-Absorbing Phenomenon

Unless the world is hit by a gigantic meteor or overwhelmed by water from melting glaciers, we can assume "big data," as the world has come to call the cascades of electronic input collected from digital devices around the world, is here to stay. The onset of big data put much attention on the importance of numbers and the skills of quantitative researchers, and in response, qualitative researchers felt the need to justify their existence and their attention to the unique narratives with which they deal. For this reason, we've heard talk about "big data" (massive numbers) and "little data" (qualitative data). However, I would suggest that instead of this pair of opposites, we might instead discuss the pairing of "big data" and "deep data."

Big data has need for those who traffic in deep data. As those who work with numbers find patterns, conflicts, anomalies, and absences in looking across vast numerical landscapes, there is equal need for those who look locally, specifically, and at the unique incident, as one does in qualitative research. Again, this suggests the need for transdisciplinary approaches that bring together quantitative and qualitative researchers around problems to which they can both contribute—team-based research is the natural answer.

## New Forms of Writing Will Continue to Evolve in Response to Digital Possibilities

Writing forms began to evolve quickly with the introduction of computers and word processing, and even faster with the advent of the internet. From formal letters we have shifted to email, and then to Twitter; from newspaper columns we have evolved to blogs and Instagram; from shopping malls we have moved to shopping on Amazon and digital wish lists. We are able to instantly update, send, or review. We can assume that our writing forms will continue to change as digital life moves forward.

One place we see this is in the forms, distribution, and assessment of research writing, which are undergoing revision as we learn to make sense of the offline and online worlds of literacy. For instance, digital capacities led to formulas for measuring the impact status of professional journals, leading to new ways of evaluating academic productivity. At the same time, various professional fields have called for faster publication venues and new review structures to make important information available in a more timely way than traditional publications could provide.

Interestingly, the increase of the digital in writing may also be leading us toward new openness and merging what had formally been two distinct worlds of writing—fiction and nonfiction. What was once anathema in traditional academic reporting (for instance, the use of "I," or the use of personal description) has gradually been creeping into social science materials (Davidson, 2012).

Social media—from Facebook and Twitter to Tumblr and Pinterest—may seem to many to be distant and apart from the serious world of research and the production and release of research results. In today's world, however, this circumstance is rapidly changing as social media become a form of research data and representation or dissemination. Social media can serve as critical locations for understanding the emerging truths of our age, as individuals of all ages, positions, and geographical locations take to the internet to share their ideas. Such studies may incorporate understanding of individuals' and groups' online and offline identities, practices, and contexts. This means qualitative researchers working on complex qualitative research teams will undoubtedly at some point need to engage with these tools as data or dissemination.

A compelling example of this issue is found in the Global Social Media Impact Study conducted by Daniel Miller, an anthropologist, and his circle of graduate students, who undertook ethnographic work on Facebook in a range of countries around the world ("Why We Post," 2016). Their study resulted in a web-based presence with blog updates on the project; hard copy and e-books, and a MOOK—meaning an online open access class that was attended by individuals from around the world; and undoubtedly numerous peer-reviewed journal articles. The project has been the source of new knowledge about social media and culture, as well as the development of new methodological techniques and the furthering of discussion about qualitative research methodology in the digital age.

Clearly, a trend of the digital world is to embed more items, meaning research tools and products, in the internet's "cloud" in different forms. This shift has multiple, layered consequences for qualitative researchers working collectively that will need to be carefully thought through.

## Issues on the Horizon

"Trends" as meant here are discussions about general directions emerging from the future, whereas "issues" are more concrete, representing what may often be looming policy changes or the formulation of standards that are almost upon us. Three issues I think will be of particular importance to team-based qualitative researchers.

### Evolving Policies of Institutional Review Boards (IRBs) and/or Similar Ethics Groups

Beginning in the 1990s, IRBs have been policy groups on steroids, evolving rapidly, their reach and influence spreading quickly within and across institutional boundaries. Few university researchers and/or those conducting research funded by governmental and private agencies can choose to ignore receiving IRB approval for their work. Today, even independent scholars are encouraged to submit their research proposals to "for hire" agencies, such as *Salus,* that will provide review and approval.

Team-based researchers operate under the same dictates as non–team-based researchers, but team-based research by its nature raises a number of new questions for IRBs. For instance, you will have multiple researchers who must obtain, and prove they have, Human Subjects Certification. Team-based research is often conducted with multiple institutional partners, and, thus, multiple IRB submissions and oversight. Team-based research may also mean multiple research sites and a corresponding need for different kinds of informed consent. Teams require training in ethics and oversight to insure ethical compliance.

Among social scientists, within institutions, and certainly from a government perspective, ethical responsiveness is an area in rapid evolution. As new forms of research continue to emerge, IRBs, and IRB policies, too, must evolve. Team-based research, being that much larger and more complicated than individually conducted research, will, in turn, absorb a correspondingly larger impact as IRBs change, grow, and develop new policies. IRBs, like big data and digital tools, are here to stay, and as such, are factors to which team-based researchers must attend.

## Institutional and Governmental Calls to Archive Qualitative Research Data

With the advent of computers, massive statistical archives rapidly became a reality. Qualitative researchers have been slow to jump on the data-archiving bandwagon, and indeed, it was some time into the computer age before digital archiving possibilities for the various forms of qualitative data began to mature. It has been government agencies in particular that have led the charge for creating qualitative research databases. In the United States and the European Union, there are growing requirements for the archiving of data collected from government-funded projects. Researchers, archivists, and policy makers are only beginning to develop the policies for these repositories and to work through the technical and political issues related to these requirements (Davidson & Fisher, 2012).

As of yet, we lack clarity about what should be submitted and how the use of QDAS will become part of these data bases. If QDAS are to be included, a first step in this direction is the development of standards by which QDAS e-projects will be designed and evaluated.

As with many arenas in qualitative research, moving from individual to team-based research, is not just an increase in numbers, but also an increase in complexity. When working with team-based research, there will be more data to submit, created by a larger number of researchers, possibly working in diverse languages, and perhaps under different institutional or national policies.

Policies for archiving data will be interrelated to other components of the conduct of research. For instance, data-archiving policies must be closely aligned with IRB policies. If interviews are to be stored in perpetuity, participants must understand how this will be done and what this will mean to them. When conducting research on a team, often in multiple locations, all team members must themselves understand what a qualitative research archive is, creating a need for yet another layer of training.

## Evaluating Faculty Productivity

As the emphasis on productive collaboration, interdisciplinarity, rigor, and research dollars increases within and without higher education, so, too, will standards for evaluation in these areas. Interestingly, one of the key markers of faculty productivity—effective "grantsmanship"—is closely related to collaboration, as the largest grants available (from government agencies) are by definition of size and resources those that will require the most partners, meaning research collaboration. In other words, teams will apply for and secure these funds, not individuals. If qualitative researchers are to be deemed successful on this scale (i.e., how many research dollars they bring to their institution), it will be important that they participate in collaborative research activities.

One interesting facet of working in digital tools is that effort and collaboration can be visualized with many of the features of these tools, providing a quantified understanding of who did what, when, and how much was produced. Examples of this tracking include the ways different contributors can be flagged in a QDAS e-project, or the ways wiki-based tools track changes, edits, and individual contributions in a joint writing effort.

## Considerations Needing Responses as We Move Forward

Finally, there are three areas of consideration of which team-based research efforts must make sense, which I refer to as: methodological, social justice, and training the next generation, meaning insuring they have the structures and resources to build on the training we have provided to them.

### Methodological Considerations

The first of these considerations relates to the perceived power differential among quantitative and qualitative researchers. In particular, how can exploration of team processes and models provide us with new ways for practitioners of both methodologies to function together, collaborate, and produce the richest results? I would hope that qualitative researchers with their openness to the humanities and arts may be able to bring new resources for team development to the table that would help team-based research break free from some of the restrictions of the scientific approach that has dominated heretofore.

As qualitative researchers increase their participation in diverse forms of team-based research projects, they will need to stop talking in their methodological *patois* and start communicating in the *lingua franca* of a wider community. Having said that, qualitative researchers are crucial to helping shift us away from simple hierarchies of knowledge to an appreciation of local knowledge—embodied and embedded—that emerges from highly reflexive processes that counter extraction and textualization and require a cyclical, rather than a linear process of interpretation (Mauthner & Doucet, 2008).

### Social Justice Considerations

Researchers of all persuasions have an obligation to attend to the deepest and most difficult issues related to diversity and meaning-making in multicultural, multilingual, and multiracial circumstances. We have the tools to bring insight to these areas. However, conducting research that is attentive to diversity in these topical areas requires that we open our true selves and natures to scrutiny with an openness that may be unsettling. This scrutiny is not limited to review of our autobiographies and subjectivities, but requires action in regard to the policies of project work, participant relationships, institutional collusion, and larger political discourses.

Research teams, with their multiple members and potentially diverse membership, offer opportunities for deep probing of cultural, racial, and ethnic differences that might not be possible for the singleton researcher. By leveraging their diversity, teams can dig into issues that might not be accessible to individuals, obtaining feedback from members that can push the group into new spaces of understanding.

However, looking at diversity as merely instrumental would be to simply follow the colonial line of thought. Diversity is more than a feature to be exploited by first-world project leaders. In evolving research models, participants' roles are shifting dramatically from "acted upon" to "acting with." In these models of research in and for the public good, observers are engaged as protagonists in the search for social justice (Sanford & Angel-Ajani, 2008). These shifts in position, role, and research model will require corresponding shifts in thought among team members, which will require time and training. As colonialism is dismantled and the North/South global divide addressed, initiation and control of team leadership must also be reorganized (Mohanty, 2003).

## Training the Next Generation

Many who will read this book are heavily engaged in the training of the next generation of qualitative researchers or are in the process of acquiring these skills themselves. It behooves us to make sure our students are ready for the real world, meaning possessing the skills to conduct research individually and as members of a complex research team. It is not enough to train them in how to conduct qualitative research as a lone researcher; rather, they need to be prepared for the team environment as well (Wasser & Bresler, 1996).

Rising researchers should not have to go out into the wider world after receiving their graduate degree, and then have to learn the basics of leading and conducting team research by the seat of their pants. They will not be competitive. Those who do not train students to use their qualitative research skills in group projects will be failing their students, something none of us want to do. Gerstl-Pepin and Gunzenhauser (2002) describe the ways their qualitative research training did not prepare them for the messiness of participating in collaborative team-based research. They conclude that "[C]ollaborative interpretation is a performative pedagogical act," calling for recognition of the unconscious as a participant on collaborative teams (Gerstl-Pepin & Gunzenhauser, 2002, p. 141).

To shift our training paradigm will require a significant overhaul of the basic qualitative research training. First, it will require an orientation toward teamwork that embodies the principles of post-modern qualitative research, as opposed to the foundational principles of a generic brand of research grounded in a positive model (Mauthner & Doucet, 2008). Team research, like individual research, will always need to monitor patterns that become normative, to ensure that they don't enter a realm of methodological thoughtlessness.

In turn, this shift will require different kinds of textbooks, curricula, and internships, and a greater emphasis on teaching with a wide range of digital tools as part of research preparation (Paulus, Lester, & Dempster, 2014). QDAS were built for lone researchers working (if on the same site) side-by-side on computers that were not yet networked. Today, these software packages struggle to reinvent themselves as networked, collaborative platforms. The need for these new forms of tools has outstripped the capacity of developers, who are working hard to catch up.

The issue of training the next generation of researchers to be able to thrive in these new environments is not restricted merely to research methodology classes and field experiences, but must also encompass overall program design, forms of advisement and mentoring, and, in particular, approaches to the key task of a graduate program—the development of the most complex and difficult levels of writing skill. We are fortunate that rhetoric or writing studies have been developing in parallel directions with the trends described here in qualitative research. There is an increasing amount of hard information available on concerns related to collaborative writing in doctoral programs and the creation of the dissertation that can be drawn upon (Bommarito, 2015; Ede, 1990; Reither, 1989; Van Steendam, 2016).

On a personal note, over the years, I have struggled to bring my qualitative research methods class closer in line with a truly team-based model. In the early years, this meant many opportunities for collaborative reading of student-produced documents—interview transcripts, observations, memos, papers, and NVivo e-projects. Students would use a variety of approaches for providing feedback to each other, as well as being asked to reflect on the quality of the collaborative processes in which they engaged. It was only fairly recently, however, that I was able to design a group project to include all class members as participants on the same research project.

Dubbing it the "Through Their Eyes" project, I implemented it in the spring 2015 and 2016 semesters. For this experiment, I paired my doctoral class with an undergraduate writing class. My doctoral students were investigating the question, "What are the transitional challenges facing undergraduates entering our campus?" The undergraduates, who were also writing about issues related to this topic, agreed to provide data to my students in the form of an interview, photos, narrative, and other writing assignments. Setting up both classes with overlapping assignments meant that there was value to both, as the meetings between undergraduates and graduates counted for both as legitimate coursework. Overlapping the times of the two classes also made the project easier to conduct. My doctoral students had only to go down two floors to another classroom (during our normal class time), an incredible savings in time for these hardworking professionals. I was lucky to have two enormously supportive colleagues working with me (Ann Dean, director of the First Year Writing Program, and Jeffrey Van Der Veen, writing instructor).

Undergraduates and doctoral students were very positive in their evaluation of the experience, but as the ringmaster of the two semester-long events, I can attest that while moving from a lone researcher model to a paired class- and team-based model was extremely rewarding for me personally, allowing me to test many of the ideas I present in this book—it was also very challenging. At this point in time in our university, program structures, class schedules, and expectations of students favor the lone researcher model, despite the fact that the institution as a whole is trying to move away from this model. In the appendices, you will find a copy of my syllabus and schedule, which will provide more information on how the experiment was structured. I hope my example will encourage others to push forward with these experiments to develop instructional plans that provide qualitative researchers with hands-on, team-based opportunities from the very beginning of their training.

## Structures and Resources

Of the trends, issues, and considerations mentioned in this section, many will require organizational attention to be solved, meaning the reworking of structures and the reallocation of resources. If my institution, the University of Massachusetts–Lowell, is any indication of the mainstream, then I would say higher education is rapidly shifting to prioritize collaboration and interdisciplinary work. Along with this shift comes greater support for nimbleness in responding to opportunity, a quality that makes it easier to act on ideas that call for team-based work.

Where universities and others may need to deploy more resources to support team-based work is in the arena of professional development around project management, digital tools, and support for writing growth. On our campus, faculty writing workshops have not only served as opportunities to increase literacy skills of different sorts, but by bringing diverse faculty together, they also offer ways to initiate future team-based work with trusted colleagues.

Literary forms and communication channels are rapidly evolving in our digital world. Although universities still privilege the peer-reviewed journal article, there are increasing challenges to its premiere place in the hierarchy of dissemination choices. It makes sense that we keep an open mind to the new possibilities for sharing knowledge with colleagues, policy makers, and the general public. Research teams can play important roles in supporting diverse literary experimentation. To make it worthwhile for them to move into these arenas, they will need the support of their sponsoring organizations.

## Closing Points

Qualitative researchers, like other knowledge workers, occupy the intersection of multiple forms of modern change. From digitalization to globalization, from modernity to post-modernity, from industrial societies to sustainable, digital societies—we struggle as individuals, members of institutions and nations, and workers who seek to bring illumination to the problems of our times.

Our work tools, whether the lead pencil, the camera, or the digital pixel, are embedded in the symbol-making of human culture; that is, the creation of texts that capture moments of social practice, which can then be analyzed in relationship to their embedded meanings. Writing, in the broadest sense that it can mean in regard to the creation of texts, is at the heart of what it is to be a qualitative researcher. We collect, make, and review narrative texts throughout the course of a project, building interpretation in multiple thin layers, like paint applied to canvas or wood.

In the conduct of qualitative research, we are always in the process of writing, whether that means developing a proposal, writing field notes, taking and sending photographs, coding materials, producing memos, or writing a book. Whether on the computer or off, writing is our central practice. What writing means to our field has changed remarkably since the time we could be officially labeled as qualitative researchers to the present. Despite the different equipment, technologies, or spatial arrangements (virtual or face-to-face), under the surface, much has remained the same. As writers of different kinds of "texts" (two-dimensional, auditory, or other sorts of visual), we still seek to understand human experience in social contexts; we still must observe, make note of, document, and collect that experience; we still separate these experiences into components, review, compare, and reorganize them to illustrate our emerging interpretations of the events; finally, we have continued to curate and compose products that temporarily fix our understanding of the events.

Various philosophies shape our beliefs about what tools we should use, what constitutes a text, how analysis should be undertaken, and what standards our final products or descriptions of our work should meet. Qualitative researchers approach this work from realist or constructivist points of view; some read like scientists and others like artists. You can argue about grounded theory versus phenomenology or case study versus narrative analysis until the cows come home—and when I write this, I truly have a picture in my head of my grandparents' small farm in Longview, Washington, and their milk cows butting heads against the white picket fence as they waited for my grandfather to come out and start the milking! Cows aside, no matter what the approach, as qualitative researchers, we write—that is, we create texts, review them, create new texts, and argue through our texts about the best approach. In the end, it all comes back to this immense amount of writing. All qualitative researchers, despite their specific approach, must also face the drum-roll of changing times and challenging new expectations.

This book focuses on one trend in our field that cannot be ignored—the increasing expectation qualitative researchers will be engaged in team-based research projects. While the notion of "team" may take many forms and include individuals in diverse roles, all teams can be understood to represent greater amounts of complexity in regard to the research act. For teams engaged in the conduct of qualitative research, writing will be the tool by which you organize, strategize, and communicate. Writing will also add to the amounts of materials, messages, and possibilities. As in all qualitative research, however, writing on projects, whether individual or team-based, is central to the capture and understanding of experience—you can't get away from it, no matter which way you turn. With all this writing comes the excitement of engaging with narratives—yours and your teammates'—as well as yours and theirs—researcher and researchee (however these roles are conceived or divvied up).

Throughout this book, despite the need to address the less romantic nuts and bolts of project work, I have tried to put the excitement of writing front and center. Qualitative researchers, I believe, have one of the best possible jobs because we do a kind of work that calls for so many different kinds of writing. Some people call this "work." Personally, for me, it's like a lifetime of indulgence in one of my greatest pleasures. Although I have conducted interesting research as a singleton researcher, I cherish the time I have worked on teams as a qualitative researcher, where I could connect to colleagues of many different sorts, consider problems of diverse nature, and share my views and experiences.

In today's world, where we live in knowledge-rich and increasingly interconnected modes, such notions as research, researcher, and researchee (or participant) are all ideas in transition within a world where distance, time, and relationship are undergoing vast changes. Traversing this landscape is an ongoing experience in the exercise of human symbol systems. Qualitative researchers with their special experience in studying, interpreting, and creating with these symbol systems bring important skills to the work of collaborative research teams.

## References

Bommarito, Daniel V. 2015. "Collaborative Research Writing as Mentoring in a U.S. English Doctoral Program." *Journal of Writing Research* 2 (2): 267–299. doi:10.17239/jowr-2016.08.02.04

Davidson, Judith. 2005. *Genre and Qualitative Research Software: The Role of "The Project" in the Post-Electronic World of Qualitative Research.* Presentation at the 2005 annual meeting if the American Educational Research Association, Montreal, Canada.

Davidson, Judith. 2012. "The Journal Project and the I in Qualitative Research: Three Theoretical Lenses on Subjectivity and Self." *Qualitative Report* 17 (6): 1–13. Retrieved from http://www.nova.edu/ssssQR/QR17/davidson.pdf

Davidson, Judith, and Joseph Fisher. 2012. "Archiving Qualitative Research Data: The Volcano Is Erupting!" QSR NVivo Trainers Conference, Cambridge, MA, August 4, 2012.

di Gregorio, Silvana, and Judith Davidson. 2008. *Qualitative Research Design for Software Users.* Maidenhead, UK: Open University Press.

Do, Jaewoo, and Lisa Yamagata-Lynch. 2017. "Designing and Developing Cell Phone Applications for Qualitative Research." *Qualitative Inquiry* 23 (10): 757–767.

Ede, L. S., and A. Lunsford. 1990. *Singular Texts/Plural Authors: Perspectives on Collaborative Writing.* Carbondale, IL: Southern Illinois Press.

Gerstl-Pepin, Cynthia I., and Michael G. Gunzenhauser. 2002. "Collaborative Team Ethnography and the Paradoxes of Interpretation." *International Journal of Qualitative Studies in Education (QSE)* 15 (2): 137.

Leavy, Patricia. 2011. *Essentials of Transdisciplinary Research: Using Problem-centered Methodologies.* Walnut Creek, CA: Left Coast Press.

Mauthner, Natasha S., and Andrea Doucet. 2008. "'Knowledge Once Divided Can Be Hard to Put Together Again': An Epistemological Critique of Collaborative and Team-Based Research Practices." *Sociology* 42 (5): 971.

Mohanty, Chandra Talpade. 2003. *Feminism Without Borders: Decolonizing Theory, Practicing Solidarity.* Durham, NC: Duke University Press.

Paulus, Trena, Jessica Nina Lester, and Paul G. Dempster. 2014. *Digital Tools for Qualitative Research.* Thousand Oaks, CA: Sage.

Reither, J., and D. Vipond. 1989. "Writing as Collaboration." *National Council of Teachers of English* 51 (8): 855–867.

Sanford, Victoria, and Asale Angel-Ajani, eds. 2008. *Engaged Observer: Anthropology, Advocacy, and Activism*. New Brunswick, NJ: Rutgers University Press.

Van Steendam, E. 2016. "Editorial: Forms of Collaboration in Writing." *Journal of Writing Research* 8 (2): 183–204. doi:10.17239/jowr-2016.08.02.01

Wasser, Judith Davidson, and Liora Bresler. 1996. "Working in the Interpretive Zone: Conceptualizing Collaboration in Qualitative Research Teams." *Educational Researcher* 25 (5): 5–15.

"Why We Post." 2016. https://www.ucl.ac.uk/why-we-post.

# Appendix A

## EXAMPLE OF METHODOLOGICAL WRITING

*Focus Group— How to Conduct*

**Focus Group Data Collection Protocol**

Building a Prevention Framework to Address Teen "Sexting" Behaviors
J. Davidson: University of Massachusetts–Lowell (UML)

### At the Meeting

As participants enter the focus group room, you will greet them, identify them, and hand them their packet (number card and questionnaires identified with case number).

Ask each participant when they take their seat to turn their packet over and wait to fill them out, which they will do as a group. Participants should put the card with their number on the table where it can easily be seen.

## Introduction to Group

***[No Recording Yet!]***

- Facilitators introduce themselves to the group
- Review the goals of the project and the ways this activity supports those goals

   **Sample Script**

   *Thank you for your participation in this research project. The goal of this project is to learn more about the issues of Teens and Sexting.*

   *We are particularly interested in learning about teens' perspectives on this issue, and we want to compare their views with the views of adults.*

   *Sexting is an issue of growing concern in our society. Yet there is little research information about this topic. This project will help provide information to those who are concerned about how to keep teens safe.*

- Review the informed consent information.
   Youth participants and some parents will have already signed informed consent forms. Other parents and the other adult group will probably review the consent forms at the meeting. In this case, you will need to review the form with them, explaining and answering questions.
   For all groups, whether or not they have already signed the form, it will be important to review critical consent information.

   **Sample Script**

   *As a participant in this study, let me remind you of your rights:*

   1. *Your participation is voluntary. You may decide at any point that you do not want to participate. You don't have to explain why. That is your business.*

2. It is our job to make sure that your materials are kept confidential. Your name will not be connected in any way to the data. You are identified with a case number. This is kept separate from the data, meaning the interview transcripts and questionnaires you fill out.
3. You will be provided with a gift card at the close of the session.

- Ask each person to briefly introduce themselves using just their first names.
- Describe the format of the session; answer any questions.

**Sample Script**

*This focus group session is scheduled to take approximately 2 hours.*

*For Students: There are three components to it—*

1. A Pre-Discussion Questionnaire
2. A Focus Group Interview
3. A Post-Discussion Questionnaire

*(For adults there are two components: Pre-Questionnaire and Focus Group).*

- Ask participants to place their Card Numbers on the table so the support facilitator can easily read them

*Pre-Focus Group Questionnaire (Youth and adult groups)*

- Ask participants to turn over their packet and select the Pre-Focus Group Questionnaire
- Distribute pencils
- Ask them to fill out just this form
- Request that they do this without speaking to their neighbor
- When completed, they will hand the questionnaire to the facilitator who will collect in the appropriate envelope
- Return pencils to facilitator

**Conduct Focus Group Interview**
- Explain to the group that you will now begin recording the session

*[Recording Begins NOW, and Use of Session Log Note the Time When the Tape Begins]*
- Pass out copies of the **Ground Rules** to focus group participants
- Review the **Ground Rules** with the group
- Ask if there are any questions before they begin

*Lead Facilitator* will ask questions, identify speakers (by number!) and probe for more information as needed.

*Support Facilitator* will be in charge of the audio recording devices and the Focus Group Log. Support Facilitator will note the number of the speaker and the first three words of their statement. Support Facilitator will also periodically note the times along with the statements.

At the conclusion of the Focus group discussion, the Support Facilitator will turn off the audio recording devices. Note the time when this is done.

**Tell the group: "We are no longer recording."**
*Post-Focus Group Questionnaire:*
- Explain to students that there is one more task to be done
- Ask them to turn over the post-focus group questionnaire; redistribute the pencils
- Ask that everyone do this on their own without discussion with others
- Provide them with time to complete the questionnaire; when completed, collect in the appropriate envelope

**Conclusion**
- Thank participants
- Distribute gift cards
- Remind them that this project will help us to provide schools, police, and others with information that will help them to create better approaches to dealing with youth and social media

# Appendix B

# FOCUS GROUP

## *Ground Rules*

- During the discussion, identify yourself by your number. For example, "Hi, I'm #1 and I think . . ."
- DO NOT refer by name to yourself or to other participants in the room.
- Because we are recording, speak in a loud, clear voice.
- The facilitator has specific questions prepared for the discussion, so please allow them to lead the discussion.
- If you wish to speak, raise your hand, and the facilitator will call on you.
- Please do not interrupt or talk over others.
- Please, no cross-talk—that is, shifting the conversation toward one-on-one discussions with others in the group.
- We ask you **not** to speak about your personal, private experiences in the Focus group. If you do so, we will

remind you of this rule and direct the conversation toward safer ground.
- We ask that what you hear here, stays here. Please respect the confidentiality of the other participants.
- There are no right or wrong answers here. We are interested in your views.

# Appendix C

## EXAMPLE OF A METHODOLOGICAL LOG

A Methodological Log is created by the researcher to track the research process. This is an example from a project created in NVivo Software.

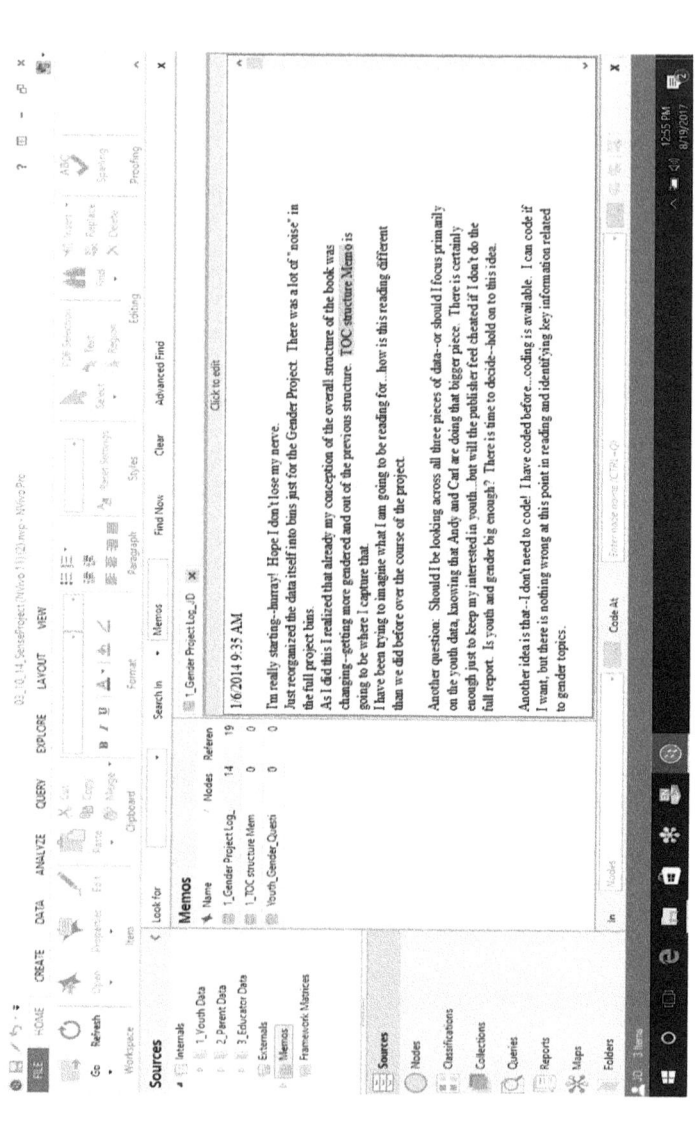

# Appendix D

## EXAMPLE OF AN EVENT LOG

This is an example of a project event log created by NVivo Software. The project event log automatically tracks all technical changes made to the project. This makes it different from the methodological log that an individual researcher would create to track the research process as seen through the eyes of the researcher.

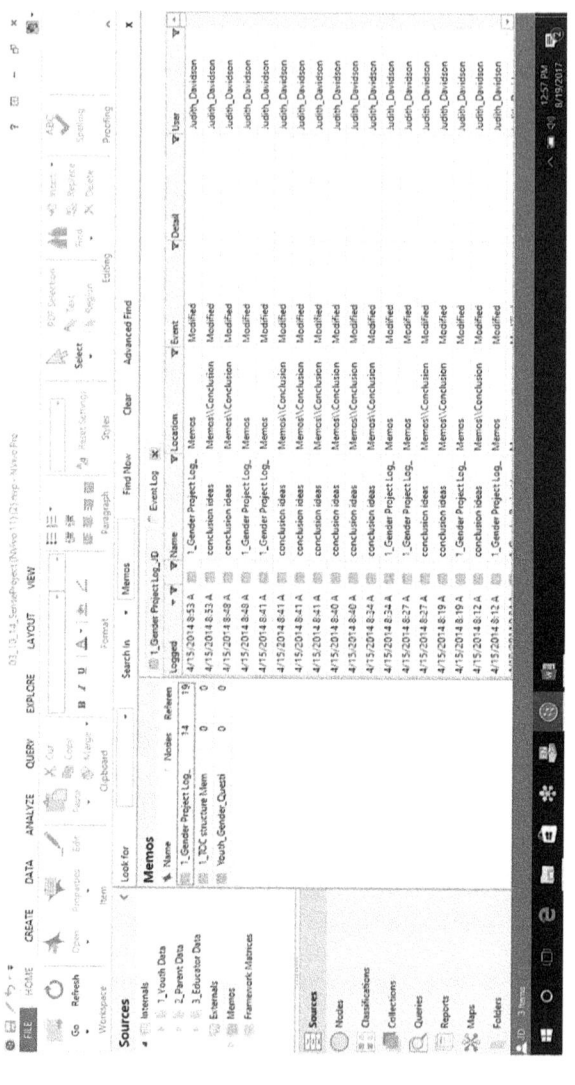

## Appendix E

# EXAMPLE OF METHODOLOGICAL CODING

I use the Gold Dust Code as a place to save items that I think will have value for future writing. I consider this a form of methodological coding. My thanks to my friend and long-time collaborator Silvana di Gregorio for coming up with this great term. This example is from a project created in NVivo.

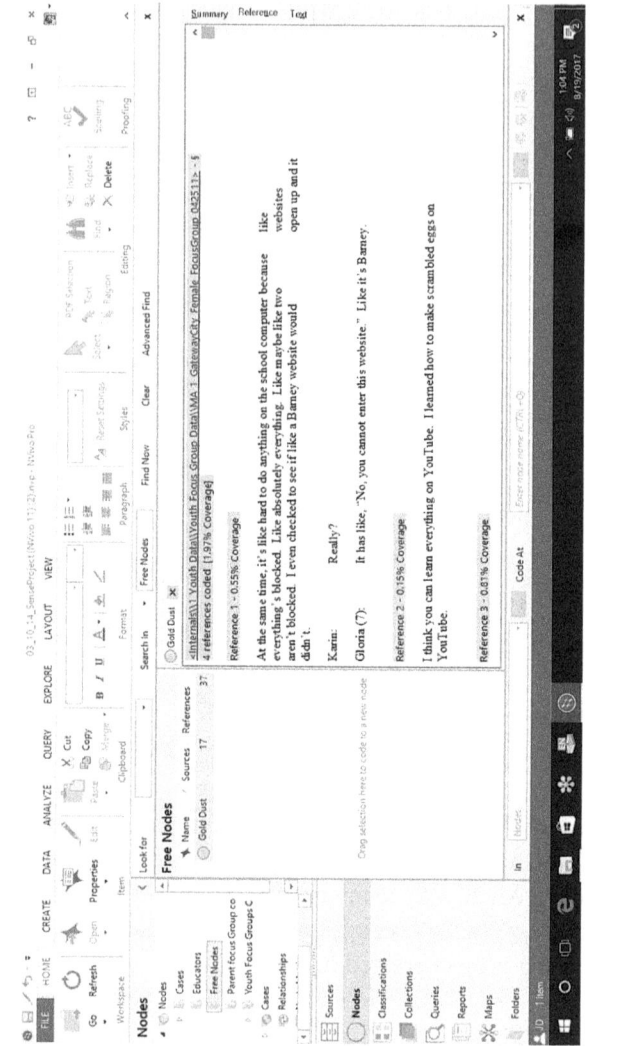

# Appendix F

## EXAMPLE OF E-PROJECT FROM THE TOP DOWN

### *Overview of Coding Section of a Project*

This is an overview of the coding section of an e-project created in NVivo. This project eventually became a book titled *Sexting: Gender and Teens* (Davidson, 2016). The codes seen here have been applied to focus group data collected from educators and other adults who worked with teens.

Reference

Davidson, J. 2016. *Sexting: Gender and Teens*. Rotterdam: Sense Publications.

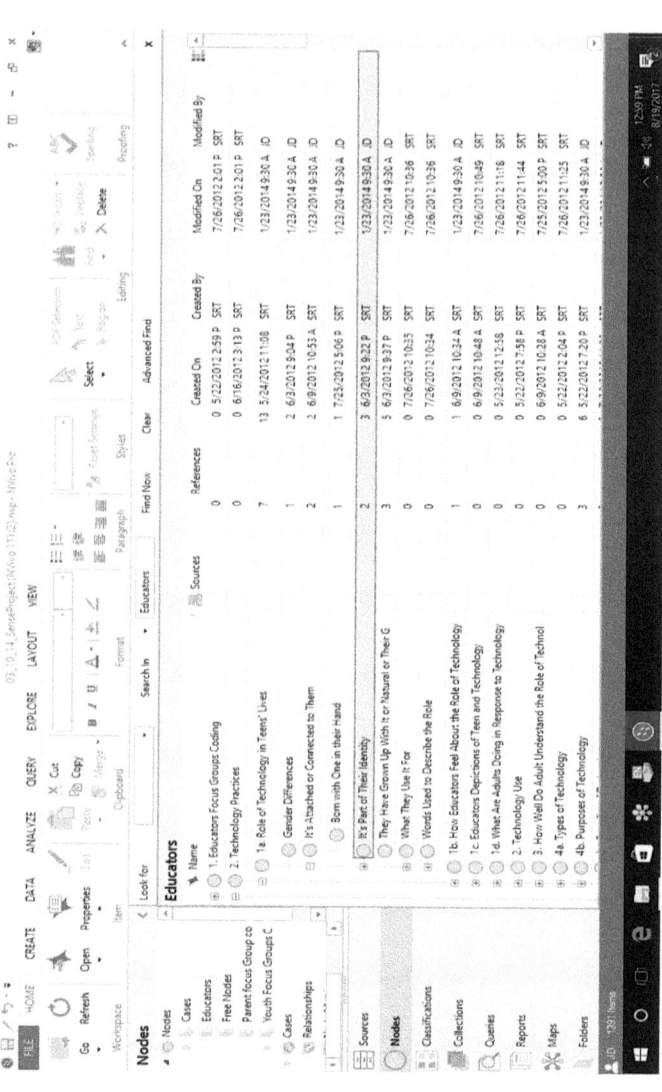

# Appendix G

# EXAMPLE OF A QUALITATIVE RESEARCH SYLLABUS

*TEAM-BASED PERSPECTIVE*

**Qualitative Research Methods: Spring 2017**

**Course Description and Goals**

The purpose of this course is to introduce doctoral students to the field of qualitative research and prepare them in the skills, techniques, and knowledge necessary to undertake independent research using this methodology, as well as to contribute to diverse research teams employing qualitative research methods.

Key topics students will be introduced to include:

Research Design in Qualitative Research
Ethics in Conducting Research with Human Subjects and Considerations of Subjectivity
Organization and Management of Qualitative Research Projects
Use of Digital Tools in Qualitative Research
Approaches to Data Collection
Analytic and Interpretive Strategies for Qualitative Research Materials
Understanding of Issues Related to Quality or Trustworthiness of Results
Methodological Literature
Representation and Presentation of Research Interpretations
Historical and Philosophical Development of the Field

In keeping with current qualitative research practice, this class emphasizes the deep understanding of ethical issues, the conduct of qualitative research as a complex team activity, and the use of a broad range of digital tools for the management and conduct of research. These emerging concerns of qualitative research are contextualized within the classic concerns of the methodology; that is, the unique paradigm that qualitative research represents and the methodological narratives that have evolved over the course of its history (e.g., ethnography, case study, phenomenology, etc.).

## Engagement in Real Research: "Through Their Eyes..."

The vehicle for our course journey will be a collaborative research project. For the purposes of the Spring 2017 semester, this research project is named "Through Their Eyes: Understanding the Undergraduate Perspective on the Transition to College."

Graduate students in the course will serve as members of a qualitative research team investigating the preselected campus issue. Our class will meet four times with an undergraduate class writing class (during a portion of our regular class meeting time) to collect data in the form of a demographic survey, face-to-face interview, drawing data exercise, and photo-voice experience. We will also gather document data from undergraduate class participants in the form of the syllabus and assignments.

The study of this problem will provide graduate students with the opportunity to experience qualitative research hands-on in real time as they are guided through the research process by the instructor. In addition, the work you do in this course will contribute to improving campus life for undergraduate students.

In Spring 2016, this doctoral level qualitative research course conducted the first "Through Their Eyes" study. You will have an opportunity to learn about that work and compare your results.
***This class will also be used for research purposes.***
In addition to serving as research assistants, you will also experience research as a research participant in this class.

Participation as a class research participant is entirely voluntary, but you are still required to complete all course assignments whether or not you want to participate in the research. If you agree to participate, these are the research data that will be collected from you:

1. A demographic survey
2. All course assignments and related artefacts
3. An email follow-up interview to be administered after the conclusion of the course

Working with the UML Institutional Review Board, I have carefully devised a process to keep your decision about participation private until after the course is completed. In this way, you can be assured that your decision will not have any bearing on your grade for the course. At the beginning of the semester, each student will be asked to sign an informed consent form that will be kept private from the instructor and held in the office of the Dean of the Graduate School of Education. At any time during the semester, students can withdraw their participation by contacting the Dean of the Graduate School of Education, who will be holding the Informed Consent forms until after final grades have been submitted to the registrar. After final grades have been submitted, I will review the informed consent forms to verify which students have granted their permission and which students have declined to participate. If you declined to participate, all of the materials you submitted for class assignments will be extracted from the pile for future study.

REMINDER: While students are not required to participate in the survey or having their coursework used for research purposes, they are still required to submit all assignments as required for the course, whether related to research or not.

Full details on the research component of the course will be provided in the Institutional Review Board (IRB) documents that will be shared with you and through the Informed Consent process.

### Required Texts

We will be using Maggi Savin-Baden and Claire Howell Major's text: *Qualitative Research: The Essential Guide to Theory and Practice* (Routledge, 2013). The paperback version is available from the bookstore.

You will also have access to hard copy and online materials about qualitative research organized that I will make available to you in class or through our Blackboard space.

In addition, you will be writing, producing, and sharing your work, as is normal in a collaborative research project. These materials will also be important components of the reading in this class.

### Required Digital Tools

In this class we will be using a Qualitative Data Analysis Tool called NVivo. UMass Lowell has a site license tool for this product that makes it free for our graduate students to use. It can be downloaded from the Information Technology site.

During the semester, I encourage you to share information about applications, software, and hardware that can help us to work smarter as qualitative researchers.

### Grading System

You will find my grading system differs considerably from the old-fashioned "points off" approach. I will be using a modification of what is called Specifications Grading. This is a grading system that focuses on competency. All students are expected to meet basic competency in all required class tasks (basic competency is a B or higher). If you can't achieve a "B" or "pass" on the task, it is my belief that you have not achieved competency in that area. A student who fails to achieve competency in the key tasks of the course (those required for a B for the overall course) fails the overall course. [That sounds harsh now, but as we go forward I think you will find it makes sense—and a B is really only basic understanding and meets all required specifications. The pass is really a very elementary level of skill.]

This is also a system that acknowledges the only way to learn more is to do more. This is why, in regard to the overall grade, students have the choice to do more or less in certain course requirements. More work will lead to a higher overall course grade, signifying the acquisition of greater skills and knowledge. Less work will lead to a lower grade . . . you get the idea.

In Specifications Grading, there is no shame in deciding you want a B or A-, instead of an A or A+. Rather, doing less work is like being employed fewer hours. On most research projects, staff are employed at varying amounts—some are full-time, some half-time, and some work even smaller portions of time. When you choose your grade, you are choosing how much time you have to give to the project.

## Kinds of Assignments

### Common Expectations

All students must meet a set of common expectations. These expectations are requirements for the Grade of B. These include the following:

- Have no more than 2 excused absences and no pattern of tardiness
- Obtain Human Subjects Certification in a timely manner
- Complete all reading assignments and participate in class discussions
- Participate in all four joint classes with undergraduate students

- Collect data from our paired class in the forms of:
  - demographic survey
  - interview
  - visual data (drawing and photographic)
  - artifactual materials (syllabus, assignments, etc.)
- Complete the methodological work assignment for the interview data
- Participate in a small group presentation to the larger group related to class technologies
- Work with class colleagues to interpret data, develop and present findings to course leaders
- Submit weekly update memos (required for 9 out of 14 weeks—see class schedule)
- Submit a final e-project for evaluation
- Submit a final reflective memo on the class experience

## Human Subjects Certification

All students in this class must obtain Human Subjects Certification. I must be provided with your valid certification so I can submit it to the IRB of UMass Lowell. Do this immediately if you do not already have the item. The UML IRB web page will provide with a link to the National Institute of Health (NIH) certification.

You will provide me with a digital copy as an email attachment. You will also store a digital copy of your certification in your e-project.

**No student in this class can conduct human subject research without having valid certification. If you have not obtained valid certification by our first joint class (Week 4: 2/8/17), I must ask you to withdraw from the class, as you will not be able to participate in the collective research activities.**

## Weekly Update Memo

Each week, regardless of what other assignments are due, you will submit a weekly update memo in which you will provide me with information on what you accomplished over the last week, the challenges you encountered, and what you have learned that is of significance to you. A critical component of this weekly update memo will be reflection on your subjectivity and positioning in regard to the research project and its participants (this will be explained in class).

This reflective memo will be approximately 500–750 words in length. It will be submitted to Blackboard (not in your E-Project), but I will also ask you to store it in your E-Project for documentation.

***The Weekly Update Memo must be submitted by no later than 9:00 a.m. on Wednesday (the day of our regular class meeting) in the appropriate Blackboard Dropbox.***

The weekly update memo is what I would expect of you if you were a paid or volunteer member of a qualitative research team I was directing. Each week I will read them in preparation for our Wednesday afternoon meeting. This will provide me with the information I need to update, tweak, and move our collective research efforts forward.

There are nine weeks that the weekly update memo will be required. There are five weeks when you are not required to submit the memo (3/8/17, 3/29/17, 4/5/17, 4/19/17, and 4/26/17). Please see the course schedule for more information on the exceptions.

## Data Collection

There will be opportunities to engage in the collection of four different data forms in this class:

- Demographic surveys
- Face-to-face interviews
- Visual data in the form of photographs and drawings
- Artifactual data

Each form of data will require different kinds of preparation and processing. In this class you will learn the opportunities and challenges each form of data raises for qualitative researchers and how to make good use of a range of data forms. This will provide you with the skills you will need later on in your program (or on other research projects) where you must decide what forms of data to use, and explain why.

Although our hands-on research project does not provide us with a formal observational opportunity, we will use a variety of resources to learn about the ways to use observations in qualitative research.

## Small Group NVivo Skill Presentation to Larger Group

Students will be divided into small groups to develop a presentation for the larger class related to a specific NVivo technical component. There will be three areas: Linking, Coding, and Searching. Please see the class schedule for more information on when these will take place. We will discuss this assignment in class.

## E-Project Development

The "e-project" is a term used to describe the digital container created by a Qualitative Data Analysis Software tool (QDAS). In this class we will be using the QDAS tool called NVivo. This is the place where you incubate your qualitative research project. Good e-project organization will be taught, and each class member will be expected to follow general guidelines for e-project development. In this way you will be able to read class projects with ease and gain the tools you would need to develop e-projects independently in the future. In addition, there will be opportunities to learn and practice digital tool competencies required by NVivo.

"The E-Project Tells All": Using this tool, we can watch your research project grow and make sense of how you understand the work you are doing. Because the e-project is digital . . . it is portable and allows for a high level of transparency. You will be able to share it, not only with me, but also in and out of class with other classmates.

In this class, you will store all your materials in an NVivo e-project, and the e-project will serve as the final paper. It will contain everything you have done over the semester—all data collected, all coding (organization and analysis), multiple memos, weekly research updates, and human subject certification.

PLEASE NOTE: NVivo is primarily a PC-based tool. It does come in a Macintosh version, but the Mac version lacks several important functions and has glitches. The computers in the Graduate School of Education (GSE) lab are Macs with dual processors and run both versions. NVivo is also available through the virtual lab of the library that can be used with any computer platform. However, there are issues with using NVivo in the cloud, and you must be sure to store and use your e-project on a stand-alone computer. If you are a Mac user, I strongly urge you to think creatively about how to get yourself access to a PC for the semester. I have had a long relationship with QSR International, the software company that makes and markets NVivo. They are always interested in the issues UML users uncover about the software. You are important informants to their ongoing research about Nvivo!

> If you are seeking a B, A–, or A, your e-project must be submitted on 4/26/17.
> If you are seeking an A+, your e-project must be submitted on 5/3/17.
> (A separate handout will describe the requirements for the e-project.)

*Final Reflective Memo*

In all of my classes, I require a final reflective memo providing me with information on the class experience from the students' point of view. Specifications for the assignment will be made available in class.

For students seeking a B, A–, or A, this assignment is due on 4/26/17 (at the same time as the e-project). For students seeking an A+, this assignment is due on 5/3/17 (also at the same time as the e-project must be submitted).

Differentiated Assignments

In addition to the Common Expectations, there is a suite of assignments with different requirements, depending upon the grade you seek: B, A–, A, or A+.

These assignments include:

- Digital Tool Competencies
- Methodological Work
- Interpretive Work

## Digital Tool Competencies

Digital Tool Competences for the B/A–/A are closely tied to the topics of the three NVivo class presentations on Linking, Coding, and Searching. Students seeking an A+ will select and explore an advanced NVivo feature. The assignments mix hands-on work in your e-project with writing a memo about the NVivo feature under study.

| Grade Sought | Digital Tool Focus |
| --- | --- |
| B | E-Project Design, Basic Maintenance, and Application of Linking Capacities |
| A– | Focus on Coding Features: 3/22/17 |
| A | Focus on Searching Features: 4/5/17 |
| A+ | Study of an Advanced Feature: 5/3/17 |

For more information, see the Grade Specifications Table and Specifications for this assignment.

## Methodological and Interpretive Work

The methodological and interpretive assignments are closely tied to the data collection activities of the class. They will provide you with an opportunity to look methodologically (and/or interpretively) within and across forms of data. All assignments are carried out through the development of memos.

Qualitative researchers make use of memos to grow the methodological and interpretive layers of their projects. Memos are ways to identify and consolidate learning about an issue. Memos are also steppingstones in the methodological or interpretive process. Writing memos about points of interest or issues about which you have questions is a way for the researcher to move more deeply into the possibilities offered by the project and its data. As the project leader, I will direct you in regard to what I want in the memos you write about the project—what they should contain and how long they should be. This information will be detailed in other handouts.

Methodological memos will focus on the process of the data collection experience, linking it, where appropriate, to ideas discussed in the textbook and/or other sources encountered in class. (The exception is the A+ Methodological Work assignment.) Interpretive memos will focus on emerging interpretations that can be located in a particular cache of data, or through analysis across several forms of data.

|    | Methodological Memos | Interpretive Memos |
|----|----------------------|--------------------|
| B  | Methodological memo on the interviewing process: 3/8/17 | No special requirement. |
| A– | Methodological memo on the visual data collection process: 4/5/17 | Interpretive memo on interview data collected: 3/22/17 |
| A  | No special requirement. | Interpretive memo on visual data collected: 4/12/17 |
| A+ | Methodological memo reviewing three methodological articles related to a methodological theme emerging from course experience: 5/3/17 | Interpretive memo on three key themes that cut across the data you (not the class) collected: 4/19/17 |

See Grade Specifications Table AND Specific Assignment Specification Handouts for more information.

## Other Key Details

### Absences and Tardiness

Students in the Graduate School of Education may not have more than two excused absences per semester. If you are absent for any reason, please email me as soon as possible describing the problem. Because we are engaged in an active research project, I will often need to adjust responsibilities so that tasks can be accomplished whether you are present or not. For this reason, I appreciate as much prior notification as is possible.

A pattern of tardiness is considered an unexcused absence, and is not acceptable. If you are not in the class ready to begin at the time the class starts (4:00 p.m.), you are considered tardy. If you have ongoing obligations that make it difficult to be in class at our start time, then you should withdraw from the class.

Excessive absence or tardiness will be considered in the final grading and may lead to a lowered grade.

## Plagiarism and Academic Misconduct

All work you submit must be original: that is, you have taken no portion of it from the work of another without due attribution. If you are unsure about the definition of plagiarism, please refer to the University catalog. The university has a site license to the software product—Turnit-In—and you can submit materials that you are concerned about here and it will give you a report on potential plagiarism questions.

It should also go without saying that all data collected will be authentic; that is, it will not be fabricated. If you have questions about this form of academic misconduct, please refer to the UML catalog for definitions and a description of the university policies that will be followed in the event of a breach of ethics.

## Who I Am . . . and What I Bring to This Work

I am very passionate about qualitative research. I think it is a unique and important way to approach the research endeavor, one that brings important insights to many sorts of social interests and needs. I consider myself a qualitative research methodologist; that is, I am drawn to issues related to building theory and practice that guides the methodology. I have long been interested in digital tools that are used in qualitative research, as well as arts-based approaches to qualitative research. My interest in qualitative research methodology has led to my involvement in diverse sorts of projects—from technology in K–12 schools, to arts education in elementary schools and at-risk kindergartens, to views on teen sexting.

Recently I have become concerned with the gap between the ways qualitative research is taught and how it is practiced in the field. I fear that many qualitative research courses (including mine) did not do enough to prepare graduate students to understand the critical ethical issues they will face in the field nor the collaborative nature of most research work. I am also concerned that qualitative research training is falling behind in preparing rising researchers to work in digital environments. This course is part of my continuing attempts to address these issues and to insure that rising researchers will be prepared for the challenges they will meet in the future.

I am so glad you are joining me this semester. I look forward to working with you and learning about your work and interests. By the end of the semester, I hope you will be prepared with the research skills you need to take the next steps in your academic journey.

## My Personal Anti-Bias Statement

(I have adapted this statement from one adopted by the UML Psychology Department.)

I welcome, value, and respect all students, regardless of race/ethnicity, religion, immigration status, sexual orientation, gender identity, (dis)ability, or political affiliation. I denounce prejudice and bigotry. I do not tolerate harassment or intimidation of our students, no matter how larger or small, intended or unintended. I encourage students to be mindful of the perspectives of others. I invite students who feel fearful or threatened to speak to me about your concerns. In this class, we will consistently adhere to appropriate warrants or standards of evidence to inform our understanding of all people.

### Education for Transformation
### Conceptual Framework of the Graduate School of Education, University of Massachusetts-Lowell

*The central tenets of our conceptual framework are*
*Excellence, Equity, Inquiry, and Collaboration*

# Appendix H

# EXAMPLE OF A QUALITATIVE RESEARCH COURSE SCHEDULE

*TEAM-BASED PERSPECTIVE*

**Qualitative Research Methods**

EDUC 7040 Spring 2017
Course Schedule
J. Davidson

| # | Date | Task/Focus |
|---|------|------------|
| 1 | 1/18/17 | **Our First Class**:<br>Introductions: Who are we?<br>What is qualitative research?<br>Instructor Handout: Definitions, Kinds, and Principles of QR<br>Framework for Understanding Forms of QR Data<br>Goals, objectives, organization, assignments, and grading of the class.<br>+Specifications Grading<br>The textbook and the Lib Guide and how we will be using them.<br>What is the *Through Their Eyes: Understanding the Undergraduate Perspective on the Transition to College* project?<br>+Share IRB documents with students<br>+Human Subjects Certification<br>+Informed Consent Process<br>+Graduate Student Demographic Survey<br>Digital Tools for Qualitative Research<br>+Getting access to NVivo<br>+Introduction to the Sample Project<br>**Preparation for Week 2:**<br>In our textbook, read:<br>-Part I: Considering Perspectives (chapters 1–3)<br>-Chapter 21—Ethics and Ethical Approval<br>Review the IRB documents for the "Through Their Eyes" project.<br>If you do not have Human Subject Certification, you must obtain before Week 4 or you will have to drop the class.<br>Explore the NVivo 11 Sample Project<br>Weekly Update in Blackboard; must be submitted by Wednesday at 9:00 a.m. |

| # | Date | Task/Focus |
|---|---|---|
| 2 | 1/25/17 | **What is Qualitative Research, Good E-Project Design, and Starting the Project** |
| | | **Course Questions** |
| | | *Discussion* |
| | | Textbook: Perspectives and Ethics |
| | | IRB Materials |
| | | *NVivo Workshop* Part I: Basic E-Project Design |
| | | -Research design in QDAS |
| | | -What are good organization principles for an E-Project |
| | | -Importing project description and IRB materials |
| | | -Creating spaces for upcoming data and memos |
| | | -Setting up cases and attributes (use of the undergraduate demographic survey) |
| | | **Preparation For Week 3:** |
| | | In our textbook, read: |
| | | *Method Sections:* |
| | | -Chapter 22—Fieldwork, |
| | | -Chapter 23—Interviews, |
| | | -Chapter 24—Focus Group Interviews |
| | | *Philosophy Sections:* |
| | | -Chapter 9—Theoretical and Conceptual Frameworks |
| | | -Chapter 10—Case Study |
| | | -Chapter 11—Pragmatic Qualitative Research |
| | | Don't dawdle on that Human Subject Certification! |
| | | Complete components for your E-Project. |
| | | Weekly Update in Blackboard; must be submitted by Wednesday at 9:00 a.m. |

| # | Date | Task/Focus |
|---|---|---|
| 3 | 2/1/17 | **Fieldwork and Interviews** |
| | | *Preparing for Conducting Research*: <br> -Review of Informed Consent Process and tasks for first joint meeting. |
| | | *Discussion of Theoretical and Conceptual Frameworks* <br> -Case Studies and Pragmatic Approaches |
| | | *Interviews in Qualitative Research* <br> -Instructor handouts on interviews <br> -Review the interview we will be using with the undergraduate class <br> -Review process for conducting the interview; processing it; completing the interview memo assignment |
| | | -Use the same process to develop interviews for selected dissertation topics |
| | | *NVivo Group Presentations*: <br> -Assigning 3 groups: Coding Tools, Linking Tools, Search Tools |
| | | **For Week 4:** <br> Review Project Proposal and Informed Consent form and script in preparation for first joint class <br> In our textbook, read: <br> -Chapter 5—Personal Stance; <br> -Chapter 20—Time, Place, and Participants; <br> -Chapter 16—Action Research; <br> -Chapter 17—Collaborative Research |
| | | **Drop-dead deadline for Human Subject Certification submission.** |
| | | Weekly Update in Blackboard; must be submitted by Wednesday at 9:00 a.m. |

| # | Date | Task/Focus |
|---|---|---|
| 4 | 2/8/17 | 4:00–4:45 p.m.: Meet first in our classroom before walking over to the undergraduate class together. Discussion of questions related to first joint meeting What is subjectivity? How is it related to ethics? How will subjectivity be present in our first fieldwork experience? *Action Research and Collaborative Research*: -What are they and how do they correspond to the forms we have already discussed? -What features do they have that correspond (or don't) to the principles of QR? First joint class: 5:00–6:15: Doctoral students meet undergraduate students; explain the research project to them; obtain informed consent; conduct demographic survey. Short caucus afterwards to answer questions and confirm decisions. Location: TBA *Submit Demographic Survey and Informed Consent **For Week 5:** Read in our textbook: -Chapter 25—Observations -Chapter 13—Ethnography Weekly Update in Blackboard; must be submitted by Wednesday at 9:00 a.m. |

| # | Date | Task/Focus |
|---|---|---|
| 5 | 2/15/17 | Fieldwork I: Follow-up discussion of the first visit, informed consent process, and other issues.<br><br>**NVivo Group Presentation: Linking Approaches**<br>Applying Linking Approaches to your E-Projects<br><br>*What is ethnography?*<br>History of anthropology and its relationship to ethnography<br>How is it intertwined with the notion of observation?<br>How is it intertwined with the other forms of qualitative research we have encountered?<br><br>**For Week 6:**<br>In our textbook, read:<br>-Chapter 27—Data Handling and Coding<br>-Chapter 12—Grounded Theory<br><br>Weekly Update in Blackboard; must be submitted by Wednesday at 9:00 a.m. |
| 6 | 2/22/17 | **Discussion of the upcoming interview experience**<br><br>*Handling and Coding Data*<br>-What is grounded theory?<br>-How does it relate to frameworks for qualitative research?<br>-What is coding? How is it related to other components of analysis in QR?<br>-Do all forms of QR use coding? How do you analyze in different forms of QR?<br><br>**NVivo Group Presentation: Coding Approaches**<br>-Applying Coding Approaches to your E-Projects<br><br>**For Week 7:**<br>Practice conducting interview<br>In our textbook, read:<br>-Chapter 14—Phenomenology<br>-Chapter 15—Narrative Approaches<br><br>Weekly Update in Blackboard; must be submitted by Wednesday at 9:00 a.m. |

| # | Date | Task/Focus |
|---|---|---|
| 7 | 3/1/17 | 4:00–4:45 p.m.: Doctoral class meets in regular classroom prior to walking over together to the undergraduate class. |
| | | *Preparations for interviews.* |
| | | *Phenomenology and narrative approach* <br> -How do these approaches shed insight on the nature of the interview? <br> Second joint class: 5:00–6:15: Doctoral students conduct interviews with undergraduate students. Short caucus afterwards to answer questions and confirm decisions. Location: TBA |
| | | **For Week 8:** <br> For all students |
| | | *Interview Assignment for B* <br> -Process the interview following instructions <br> -Share transcript with undergraduate students <br> -Write Methodological Memo for the Interview Experience <br> -Submit interview transcript and memo to the appropriate Blackboard Assignment Dropbox by the beginning of Week 8—3/8/17 |
| | | Weekly Update Memo will NOT be required for Week 8. Transcription is very time-consuming and you will also be writing a memo about the Interview experience. This is more than enough for one week. |

| # | Date | Task/Focus |
|---|---|---|
| 8 | 3/8/17 | *Undergraduate students collect digital photos of campus locations.*<br><br>DUE: Methodological Memo for the Interview Experience<br><br>**Interpretive Meeting I**: What do we know from the interviews?<br>-Analyzing within one data form<br><br>*NVivo Workshop*:<br>-Working with interview data<br>-Sharing and critique of E-Projects<br>Discussion of how to fulfill the A– Interpretive Memo for the Interview Experience and the A– Assignment for the Digital Tools Capacities (focus on Coding Features)<br><br>**For Week 9:**<br>Read in our textbook:<br>-Chapter 26—Documents<br>-Chapter 19—Arts-Based Approaches<br>Lib Guide: Review pertinent materials.<br><br>Weekly Update Memo will NOT be required for Week 9. You have quite enough on your plates! |

| # | Date | Task/Focus |
|---|---|---|
| | | **SPRING BREAK** |
| 9 | 3/22/17 | *Undergraduate students collect digital photos of campus locations.*<br><br>DUE (for A–): Digital Tools Capacity Assignment (Focus on Coding Tools)<br><br>DUE (for A–): Interpretive Memo for the Interview Experience<br><br>Arts-Based Approaches in Qualitative Research<br><br>Understanding Visual Data and Artifacts<br><br>Preparations for Week 10 joint session focused on visual data collection<br><br>Discuss upcoming A– Assignment: Methodological Memo for Visual Data Experience<br><br>**NVivo Group Presentation: Search Tools**<br>-Applying search tools to your E-Projects<br><br>**For Week 10:**<br>Review instructions for conducting visual data assignment with the undergraduate students.<br><br>Read in textbook:<br>-Chapter 28—Date Analysis<br>-Chapter 29—Interpretation<br><br>Weekly Update in Blackboard; must be submitted by Wednesday at 9:00 a.m. |

| # | Date | Task/Focus |
|---|---|---|
| 10 | 3/29/17 | 4:00–4:45 p.m.: Doctoral class meets in regular classroom prior to walking over together to the undergraduate class. |
| | | Discuss considerations related to the visual data session with undergraduates. |
| | | Data analysis and interpretation: <br> -What do these terms mean in QR? <br> -How are they different from but related to coding? <br> -How are analysis and interpretation shaped by paradigm and theoretical framework? |
| | | Third joint class: 5:00–6:15: Undergraduate students share their digital photos and discuss with doctoral students; drawing data created and discussed. |
| | | Short caucus afterwards to answer questions and confirm decisions. Location: TBA |
| | | **For Week 11**: <br> -Organize and log all visual data collected in the class. <br> -Load visual data in your E-Project and organize in the appropriate location. <br> -Develop Methodological memo on Visual Data Experience (A– and above) |
| | | [Week 11 in class, you will have an opportunity to work on the interpretation of your visual data.] |
| | | Read in our textbook: <br> -Chapter 30—Quality |
| | | Weekly Update Memo is NOT required for Week 11. You will be organizing and conducting primary analysis on your visual data. That is a time-consuming task. If you choose to do so, your visual data memo will be due at the beginning of Week 11. This assignment is required for an A–. |

| # | Date | Task/Focus |
|---|---|---|
| 11 | 4/5/17 | DUE: Methodological Memo focus on Visual Data Work (A– and above) |
| | | *Review of third joint class session and visual data collection and discussion with research participants.* |
| | | Discussion: *What is quality in qualitative research?* (Validity/trustworthiness/goodness, etc.) |
| | | **Group Interpretive Meeting II:** What do we know from the visual data? How do we think we know it? Sharing of visual data in E-Projects. |
| | | Discussion: Fulfilling the Interpretive Memo on the Visual Data Experience (A and above) |
| | | **For Week 12:** Read in our textbook: Chapter 31—Researcher Voice Chapter 32—The Research Report |
| | | Reexamine all of the primary and secondary data from the project to date. What statements or assertions can you make using this material for evidence? What are the "hot spots"? Where are there absences? Conduct more coding in your E-Project if warranted. |
| | | Review sections of the textbook related to theoretical frameworks and kinds of qualitative research. |
| | | There will be no Weekly Update memo required for this week. |

| # | Date | Task/Focus |
|---|---|---|
| 12 | 4/12/17 | DUE: Interpretive Memo on the Visual Data Experience (A and above) |
| | | **Group Interpretive Meeting III:** |
| | | What do we think we REALLY know? What evidence do we have to support our assertions? |
| | | Identifying selected themes for final presentation. Working in theme groups to find evidence and elaborate on the theme. |
| | | Discussion: Using the output of Group Interpretive Meeting III—How to develop the A+ Assignment for the Interpretive Strand |
| | | How to develop the A+ Assignment for the Methodological Strand |
| | | *What kind of qualitative research are we?* Which of the narrative strands of qualitative research does our project most closely resemble? (Review of theoretical and philosophical strands encountered) |
| | | How will we find our voice? What forms could we use to express our knowledge? [Review of Chapters 31/32] |
| | | *Planning for our final meeting with the undergraduate class*: Listening and reciprocity. |
| | | **For Week 13:** |
| | | -Work on any outstanding assignments related to the grade you are seeking |
| | | -Work on the organization and cleanup of the E-Project |
| | | Weekly Update in Blackboard; must be submitted by Wednesday at 9:00 a.m. |

| # | Date | Task/Focus |
|---|---|---|
| 13 | 4/19/17 | *4:00–4:45 p.m.: Doctoral class meets in regular classroom prior to walking over together to the undergraduate class.*<br><br>Discussion of the interrelated notions of subjectivity, ethics, reciprocity, caring, and social justice in qualitative research. How do we bring the experience to a close? What do we want to convey to our participants?<br><br>Fourth joint class: 5:00–6:15: Undergraduates share drafts of their final papers on "Transition to Higher Education" with their doctoral partners. We celebrate our partnership.<br><br>Short caucus afterwards to answer questions and confirm decisions. Location: TBA<br><br>Weekly Update in Blackboard; must be submitted by Wednesday at 9:00 a.m. |
| 14 | 4/26/17 | **Doctoral students present findings to Project Leaders (4–4:50 p.m.)**<br><br>*Discussion of the great experiment:*<br>-The value of pairing classes as we did<br>-Issues related to specifications grading<br>-Consideration of what was learned in regard to qualitative research<br><br>**For students seeking the B, A–, or A: the final submission must be made by 4:00 p.m. 4/26/17**<br>Final Submission includes:<br>1. All assignments for the grade sought, stored within . . .<br>2. An E-Project that includes all of these materials, an up-to-date methodological log, and all of the memos, linking, coding, etc., that document the assignments<br>3. Final Reflective Memo in Blackboard assignment Dropbox |

| #  | Date   | Task/Focus |
|----|--------|------------|
| 15 | 5/3/17 | **Students seeking the A/A+ grade will submit their final project materials by 4:00 p.m. 5/3/17.** |
|    |        | All of the requirements for the B, A–, and A levels, as well as the assignments required for the A+ |
|    |        | These will be stored in an E-Project, with an up-to-date methodological log. |
|    |        | A Final Reflective Memo will be submitted to the appropriate Blackboard Dropbox. |

Thank you for a great semester!

# INDEX

"acting with" research models, 127
action, in methodological log, 76
advisory boards, expert, 82
age, positionality and, 98–99
analysis
   in complex qualitative research teams, 19–22
   in qualitative research, 29–30
   role of writing in, 22–24
Anders, Allison Daniel, 20–21
anomalies, reporting on, 104
anthropology, roots of qualitative research in, 25, 26
archiving data, 61–62, 124–25
arts-based research, 23, 106–11
asynchronous communication tools, 51–53
autobiography, positionality and, 98–99. *See also* subjectivity
autoethnography, 109

bare bones methodological description, 83, 84
Bednarek, Rebecca, 96
big data, 121
bins for methodological ideas

coding methodological issues, 77–78
development of methodological library, 79–81
methodological log, 75–77
methodological memos, 78–79
overview, 74
periodic methodological reviews, 81
self and team reviews, 81–82
semi-outsider reviews, 82
Bochner, Arthur, 109
Bresler, Liora, 19, 111
Buhlman, Beat, 43
business literature, understanding of team roles and, 42

Cabantous, Laure, 96
caring, in research design, 63–66
categorization, in QDAS database, 58–59
change, qualitative research and, 30
cheat sheet, team member, 86–87
coaches, productivity, 101
coding
   methodological, 77–78, 82, 145–46
   in QDAS database, 58–59, 80, 100

collaboration, in teams, 21
collaborative features, QDAS, 60–61
collaborative writing, 23,
    88–89, 100–2
collaborators, participants as, 103
colonialism, effects on research,
    16, 20–21
communication tools, 51–54
Community-Based Participatory
    Research (CBPR), 18
community youth services,
    research in, 1
complex qualitative research teams.
    See also methodological writing;
    research design; substantive
    writing; team formation; writing
  audience for book, 8
  big data and, 121
  calls to archive research data, 124–25
  considerations needing
    responses, 126–30
  definitions related to, 6
  evaluating faculty productivity
    and, 125
  evolving policies of ethics
    groups, 123–24
  gaps in literature on, 24
  general discussion, 10, 131–33
  goal of book, 5
  increase in importance and
    diversity, 120–21
  issues on horizon, 123–25
  literature on, 16–22
  methodological considerations, 126
  organization of book, 8
  processual issues in, 19–22
  reasons for interest in, 4
  rise in use of, 13–16
  social justice considerations, 126–27
  structural issues in, 17–18, 130
  training next generation, 127–29,
    149–61, 163–76
  trends and challenges in, 1
  trends predicted for, 119–23
complex research teams, 6. See
    also complex qualitative
    research teams

consolidation of data, 99–100
consultants
  methodological, 82
  writing, 101
course schedule, "Through Their
  Eyes" project, 163–76
creative nonfiction, 107–8
creative writing in social sciences,
  106–11, 114
credit
  dissemination agreement, 46–47
  for methodological writing, 89–90
  for substantive writing, 113–14
critical arena, testing trustworthiness
  in, 103
critical goals of qualitative
  research, 28
Curry, Leslie A., 17

data
  amount collected, 49
  archiving, 61–62, 124–25
  big, 121
  collection of, 33
  collection tools, 52, 55
  consolidation of, 99–100
  deep, 121
  elicited, 31
  empowered, 32–33
  enacted, 31–32
  extant, 31
  forms of, 31–33
  research principles, 29
  selecting methods of
    inquiry, 48–49
  Sexting Project protocol for, 145
  "Through Their Eyes" project, 155
databases
  data archiving plan, 61–62
  literature, 56
  methodological, ongoing
    development of, 79–81
  QDAS, internal organization
    of, 58–59
Davidson, Judith, 19
dead projects, 3
Dean, Ann, 126

Dedoose, 60–61
DEEP (Documenting Effective Educational Practices) project, 1
deep data, 121
descriptive arena, testing trustworthiness in, 102
descriptive goals of qualitative research, 28
design, research. *See* research design
dialogic collaborative process, 21, 96
difference, as attribute for teams, 43–45
differentiated assignments, "Through Their Eyes" project, 157–59
digitalization
  complex qualitative team research and, 15
  evolution of writing in response to, 122–23
digital storage, 53
digital toolkit
  communication tools, 51–54
  components of, 52
  data and literature collection tools, 55–57
  need for new forms of tools, 128
  overview, 50–51
  project management tools, 51–54
  Qualitative Data Analysis Software, 57–61
  substantive writing and, 113
  "Through Their Eyes" project, 152, 158
  trends predicted for, 120–21
  when evaluating faculty productivity, 125–26
di Gregorio, Silvana, 145
disciplines. *See also* complex qualitative research teams
  research conducted across, 20–21
  working the boundaries, 97–98
dissemination agreement, 46–47
dissemination tools, 54
diversity
  as attribute for teams, 43–45
  social justice considerations, 126–27

documentation, establishing expectations for, 47–48. *See also* methodological writing
Documenting Effective Educational Practices (DEEP) project, 1
Döös, Marianne, 21
Doucet, Andrea, 18, 44
drama, interrogating for meaning through, 110

education, research in, 1
egalitarian participation, 18
elicited data, 31
Ellis, Carolyn, 109
emancipatory goals of qualitative research, 28
emotional journaling, 64
empowered data, 32–33
enacted data, 31–32
Endnote, 89
epistemic reflexivity, 18
e-projects, QDAS, 90, 120–21, 147, 148, 156
ethics
  caring, 63–66
  evolving policies of ethics groups, 123–24
  methodological log and, 77
  in qualitative research, 30
ethnicity, positionality and, 98–99
*Ethnographic I, The*, 109
ethnography
  autoethnography, 109
  performative, 110
  sensory, 111
Eubanks, Dawn L., 42
evaluation
  faculty productivity, 125
  goals of qualitative research, 28
  in methodological log, 76–77
event log, QDAS, 76, 143
expert advisory boards, 82
extant data, 31
externalized caring, 63, 64–66

faculty productivity evaluations, 125
fiction, social, 108

final reflective memo, "Through Their
    Eyes" project, 157
findings
    reporting on, 104
    testing trustworthiness of, 102–3
focus group interviewing process
    data collection protocol, 135
    ground rules, 139
    overview, 49
formal ethical documents, 64–66
formal writing, 93
found poetry, 110
funded research
    ideal form methodological writing
        for, 87
    semi-outsider reviews for, 82
    standardized social science writing
        for, 105–6

Garland, Diana R., 44, 45–46
gender issues
    project management system and, 50
    working the boundaries, 98–99
genres
    non-standardized or
        creative, 106–11
    standardized social science, 105–6
    as tools for qualitative research
        writing, 22, 23
geographical diversity in teams, 43
Gerstl-Pepin, Cynthia I., 21, 128
global research teams, 14, 120
Global Social Media Impact
    Study, 123
goals
    qualitative research, 28
    substantive writing, 112–13
Gold Dust Code, 145–46
government-funded research
    calls to archive research
        data, 124–25
    ethical compliance for, 65
    grading system, "Through Their Eyes"
        project, 152–53
grantsmanship, 125
Gunzenhauser, Michael G., 21, 128

Hart, Jozella, 96
health services, research in, 1–2
higher education, research in, 1
Human Subjects Certification, 154

ICPSR (Inter-University Consortium
    for Political and Social
    Research), 61
ideal form methodological writing
    bare bones description, 83, 84
    defined, 73
    overview, 9, 83
    tips for, 86–87
image/object to write
    techniques, 111
imagination, role in research
    design, 39–40
implications, reporting on, 104
indexing, in QDAS database, 58–59
individual qualitative research, 3, 4
informal writing, 93
in-process methodological writing
    bins for methodological ideas,
        74, 75–82
    capacity for reflexivity and, 74–75
    defined, 72–73
    overview, 9, 74
inquiry, selecting methods of, 48–49
insider's understanding, 29
institutional review boards (IRBs)
    ethical compliance, 65–66
    evolving policies of, 123–24
    "Through Their Eyes" project, 154
    institutions, calls to archive research
        data by, 124–25
interdisciplinarity, 14–15, 120.
    See also complex qualitative
        research teams
internalized caring, 63–64
internal organization
    QDAS database, 58–59
    of team, 44
Internet, role in research, 15
interpretation
    in complex qualitative research
        teams, 19–22

consolidation and
visualization, 99–100
goals of qualitative research, 28
interpretive meetings, 20, 95–96
interpretive memos, 95
methodological work and, 94
overview, 94
role of writing in, 22–24
testing trustworthiness, 102
working the boundaries, 96–99
interpretive meetings, 20, 95–96
interpretive memos, 95, 158–59
interpretive writing, 20
interpretive zone, 19, 21
interpretivist framework, 28
interrogating for meaning, techniques for, 109–11
intersectionality, 16
intersubjectivity, 21
Inter-University Consortium for Political and Social Research (ICPSR), 61
interview protocols
  data collection protocol, 135
  ground rules, 139
  overview, 48–49
IRBs. *See* institutional review boards
Irish Qualitative Data Archive, 61

Jarzabkowski, Paula, 96
joint writing. *See* collaborative writing
journaling, emotional, 64

K-12 education, research in, 1

labeling, in QDAS database, 58–59
Leavy, Patricia, 108, 120
Lester, Jessica Nina, 20–21
library, methodological, 79–81
Liggett, Annette M., 17–18
literature, methodological. *See* methodological literature
literature collection tools, 52, 55–56
literature review, 81
location in project, working the boundaries, 97

logs
  methodological, 59, 75–77
  QDAS, 59, 76, 143

Malacrida, Claudia, 64
Mauthner, Natasha S., 18, 44
meaning, interrogating for, 109–11
meaning-making, 19–24. *See also* interpretation
meetings, team
  discussion of methodological issues, 77
  interpretive, 20, 95–96
membership, in complex qualitative research teams, 17
members of team
  cheat sheet for, 86–87
  differences between, 43–45
memos
  interpretive, 95, 158–59
  methodological, 78–79, 82, 158–59
  "Through Their Eyes" project, 154–55, 157, 158–59
methodological coding, 77–78, 82, 145–46
methodological library, 79–81
methodological literature
  beginning steps for sharing, 88
  defined, 73
  lack of, 4
  overview, 9, 87
  QDAS projects, 90
  writing on team, 88–89
methodological log, 59, 75–77, 141
methodological memos, 78–79, 82, 158–59
methodological reviews, 81–82
methodological writing
  early in project, 47
  example of, 135
  forms of, 72–74
  general discussion, 91
  ideal form, 9, 73, 83–87
  in-process, 9, 72–73, 74–82
  interpretive work and, 94

methodological writing (cont.)
  methodological literature, 4, 9, 73, 87–90
  overview, 9, 71–72
  ownership, 89–90
  questions related to, 6
methodology
  complex qualitative research teams, 126
  trends in, 120–21
Miller, Daniel, 123
mixed methods teams, 42, 43, 51, 120–21
modeling tools, QDAS, 100

narrative constructions, 29
naturalized contexts, 29
negotiation and dissemination agreement, 45–47
nonfiction, creative, 107–8
non-standardized social science writing, 106–11, 114
Note tool, 56–57
NVivo
  collaborative features, 60
  consolidation and visualization, 100
  e-project, 147, 148
  project event log, 143
  "Through Their Eyes" project, 152, 156

online writing support programs, 101
oppression, effects on research, 16
organizational system for project. See project management system
ownership
  dissemination agreement, 46–47
  methodological writing, 89–90
  substantive writing, 113–14

paradigm wars, 14
parallel play, 100–1
participatory models, 18, 103
Patterson, Sue E., 96
Paulus, Trena, 21
peer-reviewed journals
  ethical compliance and, 65

sharing methodological insights through, 88, 89
standardized social science writing, 105, 106
performative ethnography, 110
periodic methodological reviews, 81–82
poetry, interrogating for meaning through, 110
positionality, 98–99. *See also* subjectivity
post-colonialism, 16
post-posts, 22–23
power, in qualitative research, 30
presentations, sharing methodological insights through, 88
problem-based research, 27
procedures, working out, 48–49
process, in methodological log, 76
processual issues, 19–22
productivity coaches, 101
productivity evaluation, faculty, 125
project event log, QDAS, 76, 143
project management system
  communication tools, 51–54
  data and literature collection, 55–57
  digital toolkit approach, 50–51, 52
  overview, 49–50
  Qualitative Data Analysis Software, 57–61
project organization
  data archiving plan, 61–62
  expectations for documentation, 47–48
  overview, 47
  project management system, 49–61
  selecting methods of inquiry, 48–49
projects. *See also* project management system; project organization
  dead, 3
  defined, 7
  planning tools, 53
  QDAS, as methodological literature, 90
proximity, intersubjectivity and, 21

Qualibank, 61
Qualitative Data Analysis
    Software (QDAS)
    archiving in, 62, 125
    collaborative features, 60–61
    consolidation and visualization, 100
    e-projects, 90, 120–21, 147, 148
    internal organization of, 58–59
    methodological library, 80–81
    methodological log, 76
    need for new forms of tools, 128
    overview, 52, 57–58
    project event log, 76, 143
    projects as methodological
        literature, 90
    Reference Managers and, 59–60
    "Through Their Eyes" project,
        152, 156
    trends predicted for, 120–21
Qualitative Data Repository
    (QDR), 61
qualitative research. *See also* complex
    qualitative research teams;
    methodological writing; research
    design; substantive writing;
    writing
    analysis, 29–30
    big data and, 121
    calls to archive research
        data, 124–25
    considerations needing
        responses, 126–30
    data, 29, 31–33
    dead projects, 3
    defined, 25
    definitions related to, 6
    evaluating faculty productivity
        and, 125
    evolving policies of ethics
        groups, 123–24
    gaps in literature on, 24
    general discussion, 33–34, 131–33
    history and context, 25–27
    increased recognition of, 14
    increase in team-based, 120–21
    individual, 3, 4
    issues on horizon, 123–25
    methodological considerations, 126
    principles of, 28–30
    problem-based research, 27
    products of, 30
    research kinds, 26–27
    role on complex research team,
        40, 42–43
    social justice
        considerations, 126–27
    stance, goals, foundations, 28
    structures and resources, 130
    subjectivity, ethics, power, and
        change, 30
    training next generation, 127–29,
        149–61, 163–76
    trends and challenges in, 1
    trends predicted for, 119–23
quantitative researchers, collaboration
    with, 126

race, positionality and, 98–99
recommendations, reporting on, 104
Reference Managers
    overview, 56
    QDAS and, 59–60
reflection/reflexivity
    in-process methodological writing
        and, 74–75
    internalized caring and, 63–64
    in methodological log, 76–77
    "Through Their Eyes" project,
        154–55, 157
reporting, forms of, 103–11
repositories, data, 61–62
representational groups, 17
research design
    caring, 63–66
    data archiving plan, 61–62
    expectations for
        documentation, 47–48
    overview, 9, 28–29
    project management system, 49–61
    project organization and, 47–62
    role of writing in, 39–40, 66–67
    selecting methods of inquiry, 48–49
    team formation, 40–47
    research kinds, 26–27, 29

research teams. *See* complex qualitative research teams; team research
resources, issues related to, 130
responsive poetry, 110
results, testing trustworthiness of, 102–3
retreats, writing, 101
reviews, methodological, 81–82
roles
  in complex qualitative research teams, 17–18, 42
  in data collection, 33
  participants as collaborators, 103
  working the boundaries, 97

Salmons, Janet, 31
scaling up projects, 17
schedule, "Through Their Eyes" project, 163–76
scholarly writing. *See* methodological literature
Scobie, Willow, 75
security, digital storage, 53
self-care, 64
self-conducted reviews, 81–82
semiformal ethical documents, 64
semi-outsider reviews, 82
sensory ethnography, 111
Sexting Project
  consolidation and visualization, 100
  e-project for, 147, 148
  focus group interviewing protocol, 49, 135, 139
  overview, 1
  working the boundaries, 97, 98
shared writing times, 101
sharing methodological insights. *See* methodological literature
Siltanen, Janet, 75
sites, working the boundaries, 97
social fiction, 108
social justice, 16, 32–33, 126–27
social media, 54, 122–23
social science writing
  non-standardized or creative, 106–11
  standardized, 105–6

sociology, roots of qualitative research in, 25, 26
solely qualitative research teams, 42, 43
solo qualitative research, 3, 4
Specifications Grading, 152–53
standardized methodological description. *See* ideal form methodological writing
standardized social science writing, 105–6
Stanton, Maureen, 107–8
storage, digital, 53
structural issues, 17–18, 130
subjectivity
  internalized caring and, 63–64
  methodological log and, 76–77
  in qualitative research, 30
  working the boundaries, 98–99
substantive writing
  beginning writing process, 100–2
  conditions to ensure success, 112–14
  credit for, 113–14
  forms of reporting and kinds of writing, 103–11
  general discussion, 115
  goals, responsibilities, and timelines, 112–13
  interpretive work, 94–100
  non-standardized or creative, 106–11
  overview, 9, 93–94
  questions related to, 6
  standardized, 105–6
  testing trustworthiness, 102–3
support programs, online writing, 101
syllabus, "Through Their Eyes" project, 149–61
synchronous communication tools, 51–53

team formation
  difference as attribute, 43–45
  gathering team members, 41–42
  negotiation and dissemination agreement, 45–47

principles of, 40–41
role of qualitative research on team, 40, 42–43
team meetings
  discussion of methodological issues, 77
  interpretive, 20, 95–96
team member cheat sheet, 86–87
team methodological reviews, 81–82
team research. *See also* complex qualitative research teams; team formation
  definitions related to, 6
  evolving policies of ethics groups, 123–24
  trends and challenges in, 1
team writing, 88–89
technical log, QDAS, 76, 143
technology, 15. *See also* digital toolkit; social media
teen sexting project. *See* Sexting Project
texts, in qualitative research, 25. *See also* writing
theoretical goals of qualitative research, 28
"Through Their Eyes" project
  course schedule, 163–76
  distribution of credit, 114
  drama, use in, 110
  syllabus for, 149–61
  training next generation, 129
  timelines, substantive writing, 112–13
toolkit, digital. *See* digital toolkit
training for complex qualitative team research
  course schedule for, 163–76
  general discussion, 127–29
  syllabus for, 149–61
transdisciplinary approaches, 14–15, 120, 121–22. *See also* complex qualitative research teams
trustworthiness, testing, 102–3

University of Massachusetts-Lowell, 130. *See also* "Through Their Eyes" project

Van Der Veen, Jeffrey, 126
virtual teams, 43
visual arts, 111
visualizations
  interpretive work, 99–100
  in methodological reviews, 82

Wasser, Judith Davidson. *See* Davidson, Judith
Weaver, Tim D., 96
weekly update memos, "Through Their Eyes" project, 154–55
Wilhelmson, Lena, 21
Willis, Alette, 75
Woodside, Marianne, 21
word processing tools, 53–54
working the boundaries
  disciplines, 97–98
  overview, 96
  positionality, subjectivity, or autobiography, 98–99
  role or location in project, 97
workshops
  creative nonfiction, 107–8
  sharing methodological insights through, 88
  writing, 101
writing. *See also* methodological writing; substantive writing
  about ethics, 64–66
  about subjectivities, 64
  across disciplinary boundaries, 20–21
  changing understanding of, 22–24
  emotional journaling, 64
  evolution of in response to digital possibilities, 122–23
  expectations for documentation, 47–48
  gaps in literature on, 24
  general discussion, 10
  goal of book, 5
  interpretive, 20
  kinds of, 103–11
  methods of inquiry and, 48–49
  non-standardized or creative, 106–11
  organization of book, 8

writing (*cont.*)
   reasons for emphasis on, 9
   in research design phase,
      39–40, 66–67
   role in qualitative research, 131–32
   standardized social science, 105–6
   structures and resources for
      experimenting with, 130
   on team, 88–89
   tools to support, 53–54
   training next generation in, 128–29
   trends in, 5
writing consultants, 101
writing retreats, 101
writing workshops, 101

youth services, research in, 1

Ziegler, Mary, 21
zone, interpretive, 19, 21